Table of Contents

Acknowledgments

I would like to express my gratitude to my editor Mr. Bill Bai, as well as Mr. Hanren Tu for the contribution of their professional knowledge and endless support in completing this book.

Jacky Bai

About This Book

The goal of this hands-on book is to teach you, the reader, the ins and outs of data manipulation and analytics using Pandas. It introduces comprehensive and in-depth data analytics techniques with Pandas, and helps you quickly master data manipulation and analytical skills, whether you are new to Python or an experience data scientist using other languages.

Throughout this book, three small, carefully designed data sets are used to explain all of Pandas' functions. At the end, a detailed use case is provided to demonstrate how Pandas works with Python in real-life applications.

If you are new to data analytics, you will find that this book explains complex concepts in a simple yet effective way, assisted with visual explanations. As for those who are experienced data engineers or data scientists, this book will be your best friend when working on projects requiring Pandas. In short, this book is for everyone, regardless of skill level.

About the Author

Jacky Bai is a leading expert in business solutions and data science sources in different areas: finance, consumer marketing, healthcare, and behavioural data. He has hands-on experience in data analytics and data sciences using Python, R and SAS for over 20 years.

Jacky has a well-rounded education background and work experience in statistics, finance and computer science, which makes him a top contributor in-depth consultation helping people interactively solve complex business issues from multiple vision.

Working with researchers and industry experts, he has developed cutting-edge data-intensive applications in risk management, finance, consumer marketing, and trade surveillance areas and data fusion techniques which enable top rank financial industry clients such as banks and insurance companies to create granular and comprehensive data products.

Chapter 1. Getting Started with Python and Pandas

1.1 Python Installation

Python is a powerful, high-level, general-purpose, interpreted, and object-oriented programming language, first released in 1991. Due to its simplicity and flexibility, Python is one of the most popular programming languages as of 2020, especially in the data science area.

Before you start working on data analysis projects, you'll need Python and Pandas installed on your computer, as well as a Python IDE. The most recent stable version of Python can be downloaded from the official home of Python.

Download:

https://www.python.org/downloads/

To install Python on your machine, simply enter the link in your browser, press "Download Python", and follow the installation steps in the installer.

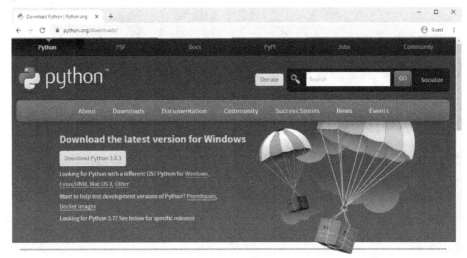

1.2 Popular Python IDEs

An integrated development environment (IDE) is an interface which provides a plethora of tools to accelerate your programming workflow. A standard IDE usually comes with a source code editor, compiler or interpreter, and a debugger. As opposed to a simple text editor like notepad, an IDE will allow you to finish projects much faster, with a variety of tools available at hand.

1.2.1 Jupyter Notebook (https://jupyter.org/)

Jupyter Notebook is an open-source web application that allows you to interactively develop and present code and its output into a single document which can contain live code, mathematical equations, visualizations, narrative text and other rich media. Currently, Jupyter supports over 40 programming languages, including Python, R, and Scala. It can be installed through Anaconda or pip.

Installation:

```
pip:   pip install jupyterlab
conda: conda install -c conda-forge jupyterlab
```

To launch Jupyter, type "jupyter notebook" into your command line, and wait for Jupyter to launch in your default web browser.

1.2.2 PyCharm (https://www.jetbrains.com/pycharm/)

PyCharm is a popular IDE used by professional developers, created by JetBrains. It supports many valuable features that a good IDE should provide: Git integration, code completion, error-highlighting and fixes, debugging, and code refactoring. PyCharm also provides backend support for major Python web frameworks such as Flask and Django, SQL support, and frontend support for HTML, CSS, and ReactJS, making it a versatile full-stack IDE for Python.

There are two versions of PyCharm:

- Community – A free, open-source, and lightweight IDE good for Python and scientific development.
- Professional – A subscription based, full-featured IDE with support for web development

Download:

https://www.jetbrains.com/pycharm/download/

Here is a look at PyCharm:

(https://www.jetbrains.com/pycharm/)

1.2.3 Spyder (https://www.anaconda.com)

Spyder, short for "Scientific Python Development Environment", is a free IDE that is included with Anaconda. It is designed as a workbench for scientific computing with Python, and works best with interactive environments that involve visualizations, graphing, and related tasks. Spyder also allows you to view the variables and results for any block of code, which is often crucial in the fields of data science, engineering, and scientific research.

Download:

https://www.anaconda.com/products/individual

A snapshot of Spyder is shown below.

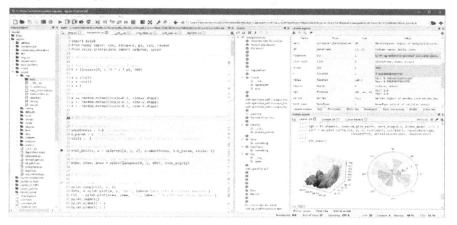

(https://www.spyder-ide.org/)

1.3 Installing Pandas

Pandas is the most important data manipulation and analysis tool available to you. To install Pandas, simply enter the command shown below into your command line.

```
pip install pandas
```

The 'Hello, World!' of Pandas

Once Pandas has been installed, you can check if it is working properly by creating a dataset and printing it out.

```
import pandas as pd
df_helloworld = pd.DataFrame (
        {'Name': ['Jacky', 'Henry'],
        'Say': ['Hello', 'World']})
print(df_helloworld)
```

out:

```
     Name    Say
0   Jacky   Hello
1   Henry   World
```

Once you've confirmed that Pandas is working, you're all set to use Python and Pandas for data manipulation and analysis.

Chapter 2. Importing and Exporting Data in Pandas

Pandas (Panel + Data) is the most important Python library for data manipulation and analysis. It is built on top of NumPy, and expands on NumPy by providing intuitive functions for data analysis. This chapter introduces data structures and data types in Pandas, methods of importing data into Pandas, and methods of exporting data out of Pandas through different data formats.

2.1 Pandas Data Structures

The two primary data structures of Pandas are Series and DataFrames. A Series is a one-dimensional array with access labels which can be indexed. A DataFrame is a 2-dimensional, labeled, SQL table-like data structure with the ability to have different types of columns, which are essentially just Series. DataFrames are the most frequently used data object in Pandas, and provide every feature that other 2-dimensional data types provide, and much more.

Series:

	0	Jacky
	1	Jane
Index	2	Henry	Data
	3	Desmond
	4	Eileen

DataFrame:

Column Name   Columns

		First Name	Last Name	Credit Score	Credit Approva	Card Name	Income	Approval Date	
	0	Jacky	White	825	TRUE	Infinite	155000.62	2019-09-13 12:00:00	
Index	1	Jane	Nize	810	TRUE	Golden	120800.88	2019-08-16 05:25:00	Rows
	2	Henry	Tone	780	TRUE	Golden	98000.58	2019-05-06 12:00:00	
	3	Desmond	Black	750	TRUE	Silver	54000	2019-05-01 01:00:00	
	4	Eileen	Musk	620	FALSE	Dividend	35000	NaN	

Data   Missing Value

2.2 Creating Data through Hand-Typing

Before doing any data-related operation using Pandas, one must first load the data into Pandas. Pandas can create Series or DataFrame objects through different methods. They can be created through manually typing the data contents from Python directly, or importing data from existing text files, database tables, or other formatted data files.

The simplest way to create a Series or DataFrame in Pandas is by manually typing the contents in Python directly. Note that this will only work for smaller datasets. Now, let's see how a Series or DataFrame is created.

A Series can be created by using the *Series()* function.

```
Series(data, index, dtype, copy)
Arguments:
    data: list, constants, or ndarray
    index: (defaulted to RangeIndex), index to use for resulting series
```

Creating a Series by list

```
import pandas as pd
s = pd.Series(['a','b','c','d'])
```

out:

```
0    a
1    b
2    c
3    d
dtype: object
```

Series may look flashy to you, but in the real world, most datasets consist of 2-dimensional tabular data, including both rows and columns which share the same properties. To analyze this kind of data, you'll need to use a 2-dimensional structure, which a DataFrame conveniently represents. Pandas can create a DataFrame from a dictionary or list using the *DataFrame()* function.

10

```
DataFrame(data, index, columns, dtype)
Arguments:
    data: dict, list, or DataFrame
    index: index to use for resulting frame, (defaulted to RangeIndex)
    columns: column names to use for resulting frame
```

Creating a DataFrame from a dictionary

When using dictionaries to create DataFrames, the keys of the dictionary will become the columns of the DataFrame, and the values will become the rows.

```
import pandas as pd
df_helloworld = pd.DataFrame (
            {'Name':  ['Jacky', 'Henry'],
            'Say': ['Hello', 'World']})
```

out:

	Name	Say
0	Jacky	Hello
1	Henry	World

Creating a DataFrame from a list

When using a multi-dimensional list to generate a DataFrame, you must specify column names for the generated DataFrame.

```
df_helloworld = pd.DataFrame ([['Jacky', 'Hello'],
                ['Henry', 'World']],
                columns = ['Name', 'Say'])
```

out:

	Name	Say
0	Jacky	Hello
1	Henry	World

11

Creating a DataFrame using a specific datatype

You can also use the ***dtype*** argument to cast the given data to a specified type in the DataFrame. In the example below, the inputted numbers are casted to a *float* datatype.

```
df_helloworld = pd.DataFrame([['Jacky', 'Hello', 28.5],
                              ['Henry', 'World', 23]],
                             columns =['Name','Say','Grade'],
                             dtype = float)
```

out:

	Name	Say	Grade
0	Jacky	Hello	28.5
1	Henry	World	23.0

2.3 Importing and Exporting External Data Using Pandas

Pandas provides a set of powerful and flexible functions to allow you to import different formats of existing external data files to a DataFrame, and vice versa. This job is done by a set of top-level Reader and Writer functions. The Reader function allows you to load files into Pandas, while the Writer function allows you to export to an external file.

All of the Reader functions follow the same naming scheme of *pandas.read_<file-type>()* to generate a DataFrame from a file containing data, and all Writer functions are object functions that use the naming scheme *to_<file-type>()*. In both methods, *<file-type>* represents the type of file that stores the data. You can add arguments in both functions to fit the external data file's options, such as *delimiter* for specifying the delimiter of a csv file, *sheet_name* for specifying the sheet needed in an excel file, and database

ODBC configurations for accessing a database. The samples below illustrate how Reader and Writer functions work.

2.3.1   Importing a CSV/Excel File

Importing a CSV file:

```
import pandas as pd
pd.read_csv('temp.csv')
```

Importing an EXCEL file:

```
import pandas as pd
pd.read_excel('temp.xlsx', sheet_name='Sheet1')
```

2.3.2   Importing database tables

Pandas also provides the *read_sql()* function to load data from an external database directly into a DataFrame. However, to perform this task, a connection between Python and the database must be established. This can be acheived using the ***pyodbc*** package. Pyodbc allows you to use a connection string variable, which includes the required database's connection information, to call a SQL query to access the data in the database.

The sample code below is used to create a DataFrame by importing data from Access and SQL Server databases, respectively. The code includes 3 parts:

1. Building the ODBC connection authentication string, conn, which specifies the database access authentication information.
2. Creating the SQL query code that defines the required data from the database, that needs to be imported.
3. Loading the queried data from the database using the ODBC connection authentication.

13

Importing from an Access database:

```
import pyodbc
import pandas as pd
conn = pyodbc.connect(
    r'Driver={Microsoft Access Driver (*.mdb, *.accdb)};
    DBQ=C:\python\mydb.accdb;')
SQL_Query = 'select * from test_table'
df = pd.read_sql(SQL_Query, conn)
```

Importing from a SQL Server database:

The authentication information of a SQL Server database includes the following information: *Server=Server; database=Database; UID=UserName; PWD=Password;*

```
import pyodbc
import pandas as pd
server = 'tcp:myserver.database.windows.net'
database = 'mydb'
username = 'myusername'
password = 'mypassword'
conn = pyodbc.connect('DRIVER={ODBC Driver 17 for SQL Server};
                       SERVER='+server+';
                       DATABASE='+database+';
                       UID='+username+';
                       PWD='+ password)
SQL_Query = 'select * from test_table'
df = pd.read_sql(SQL_Query, conn)
```

2.3.3   Importing web data files

If your data is hosted on the internet, you can create a DataFrame using the url of your file. The example below pulls a csv file from a website.

```
import pandas as pd
url= "https://raw.githubusercontent.com/billbai0102/Pandas-
Book/master/credit.csv"
df_credit = pd.read_csv(url)
```

2.3.4 Exporting Data from Python

Writer functions can export a DataFrame to a specified file format. They are very powerful and convenient, as Pandas provides many different write options for different file types, as each file type may have its own requirements. To learn about each and every option provided, refer to the official Pandas documentation, as there are dozens of different options, most of which you may not even need or use. Here are some examples of exporting DataFrames to the most commonly used file types, such as CSV, JSON, and HTML.

Writing to a CSV file

```
df.to_csv('output.csv')
```

Writing to a JSON file

```
df.to_json('output.json)
```

Writing to an HTML file:

```
df.to_html ('output.html)
```

Reader and Writer functions support many data formats. Listed below are all data formats supported by Pandas for your reference.

Format type	Data Description	Reader	Writer
TEXT	CSV	read_csv	to_csv
TEXT	Fixed-Width Text File	read_fwf	
TEXT	JSON	read_json	to_json
TEXT	HTML	read_html	to_html
TEXT	Local clipboard	read_clipboard	to_clipboard
	MS Excel	read_excel	to_excel
BINARY	OpenDocument	read_excel	

BINARY	HDF5 Format	read_hdf	to_hdf
BINARY	Feather Format	read_feather	to_feather
BINARY	Parquet Format	read_parquet	to_parquet
BINARY	ORC Format	read_orc	
BINARY	Msgpack	read_msgpack	to_msgpack
BINARY	Stata	read_stata	to_stata
BINARY	SAS	read_sas	
BINARY	SPSS	read_spss	
BINARY	Python Pickle Format	read_pickle	to_pickle
SQL	SQL	read_sql	to_sql
SQL	Google BigQuery	read_gbq	to_gbq

* A blank cell denotes that Pandas does not support the Writer function

2.4 Pandas Data Types and Attributes

When performing data analyses, it is especially important to make sure you are using the correct data types and associated functions, otherwise you may get unexpected results or errors. The table below illustrates the basic Pandas data types (aka *dtypes*), and corresponding data types in Python:

Pandas dtype	Python type	Usage
object	str	Text
int64	int	Integer numbers
float64	float	Floating point numbers
bool	bool	True/False values
datetime64	NA	Date and time values
timedelta (ns)	NA	Differences between two dates or times
category	NA	Finite list of text values or np.nan

A toy dataset will be used as an example for the following examples, showcasing the various data types in a DataFrame. You may download and experiment with this dataset by following the link provided:

(https://raw.githubusercontent.com/billbai0102/Pandas-Book/master/credit.csv).

```
import pandas as pd
url = "https://raw.githubusercontent.com/billbai0102/Pandas-
Book/master/credit.csv"
df_credit = pd.read_csv(url, parse_dates = ['Approval Date'])
```

out:

First Name	Last Name	Credit Score	Credit Approval	Card Name	Income	Approval Date
Jacky	White	825	True	Infinite	155000.62	2019-09-13 12:00:00
Jane	Nize	812	True	Golden	120800.88	2019-08-16 05:25:00
Henry	Tone	780	True	Golden	98000.58	2020-05-06 12:00:00
Desmond	Black	750	True	Silver	54000.00	2020-05-01 01:00:00
Eileen	Musk	620	False	Dividend	35000.00	

Checking data types

To see the data type of each column, use the ***dtypes*** attribute.

```
df_credit.dtypes
```

out:

```
First Name          object
Last Name           object
Credit Score         int64
Credit Approval       bool
Card Name           object
Income             float64
Approval Date  datetime64[ns]
dtype: object
```

You may also use the *info()* function to get the data types along with a concise summary of the DataFrame.

```
df_credit.info()
```

out:

```
<class 'pandas.core.frame.DataFrame'>
RangeIndex: 5 entries, 0 to 4
Data columns (total 7 columns):
First Name       5 non-null  object
Last Name        5 non-null  object
Credit Score     5 non-null  int64
Credit Approval  5 non-null  bool
Card Name        5 non-null  object
Income           5 non-null  float64
Approval Date    4 non-null  datetime64[ns]
dtypes: bool(1), datetime64[ns](1), float64(1), int64(1),
object(3)memory usage: 373.0+ bytes
```

To check the data type of a particular column, apply the ***dtypes*** attribute directly to the column.

```
df_credit['Income'].dtype
```

out:

dtype('float64')

Changing data types of columns

More often than not, you'll need convert your data from one type to another, to suit the needs of the data analysis. The *astype()* function will allow you to cast a Pandas object to another specified data type. Here is an example to convert the data type of "Card Name" from object to category.

```
df_credit['Card Name'] = df_credit['Card Name'].astype('category')
df_credit['Card Name'].dtype
```

out:

```
CategoricalDtype(categories=['Dividend', 'Golden', 'Infinite',
'Silver'], ordered=False)
```

2.4.1   The Attributes of Pandas' DataFrame

Since Pandas' DataFrame is the most important and popular data structure in data analysis, you'll need a strong understanding of its attributes.

18

The table below lists all attributes of a DataFrame, which allows you to access its underlying metadata.

Data Frame Attributes	
T	Transpose index and columns.
at	Access a single value for a row/column label pair.
attrs	Dictionary of global attributes on the object.
axes	Return a list representing the axes of the DataFrame.
columns	The column labels of the DataFrame.
dtypes	Return the dtypes in the DataFrame.
empty	Indicator whether DataFrame is empty.
iat	Access a single value for a row/column pair by integer position.
iloc	Purely integer-location based indexing for selection by position.
index	The index (row labels) of the DataFrame.
loc	Access a group of rows and columns by label(s) or a boolean array.
ndim	Return an int representing the number of axes / array dimensions.
shape	Return a tuple representing the dimensionality of the DataFrame.
size	Return an int representing the number of elements in this object.
style	Returns a Styler object.
values	Return a Numpy representation of the DataFrame.

For instance, you can access the *T* attribute of a DataFrame, which may come in handy when you need to transpose it.

```
df_helloworld.T
```

out:

	0	1
Name	Jacky	Henry
Say	Hello	World
Grade	28.5	23

As well, you can also access the ***shape*** attribute of a DataFrame to get its dimensionality. The example below shows that the DataFrame, df_helloworld, has 2 rows and 2 columns, respectively.

```
df_helloworld.shape
```

out:

$$(2, 2)$$

Chapter 3. Accessing a DataFrame

By now, you've learned about the various data structures in Pandas, as well as how to create or import data into a Pandas data structure. This book will mainly focus on the DataFrame object because of its importance and popularity in data processing. However in this chapter, you'll be taught how to obtain the basic statistics of a DataFrame, the indexing of a DataFrame, and how to use the index to access specific data in a DataFrame.

For illustration purposes, we've created a sample toy database including three datasets: credit, cards, and transactions. These examples are used to show how Pandas works with data manipulation and data analysis. Of these three datasets, *credit* mimics the customer's credit information, including customer name and credit score, *cards* mimics the customer's credit card information, including customer name and card number, and *transactions* mimics the transaction history of the credit cards, such as card number and spending amount. These three datasets are linked by the card numbers and customer names. The content of the datasets are shown below.

Credit						
First Name	**Last Name**	**Credit Score**	**Credit Approval**	**Card Name**	**Income**	**Approval Date**
Jacky	White	825	True	Infinite	155000.62	2019-09-13 12:00:00
Jane	Nize	812	True	Golden	120800.88	2019-08-16 05:25:00
Henry	Tone	780	True	Golden	98000.58	2020-05-06 12:00:00
Desmond	Black	750	True	Silver	54000.00	2020-05-01 01:00:00
Eileen	Musk	620	False	Dividend	35000.00	

Cards

First Name	Last Name	Card Number	Limitation	Effective Date
Jacky	White	CN012	10000	2019-09-13 12:00:00
Jane	Nize	CN014	9800	2019-08-16 05:25:00
Henry	Tone	CN015	12000	2019-09-13 12:00:00
Desmond	Black	CN016	5000	2019-08-16 05:25:00
Henry	Tone	CN015	15000	2020-05-06 12:00:00
Desmond	Black	CN016	2000	2020-05-01 01:00:00

Transactions

Card Number	Date	Transactions	Amount
CN012	2019-09-01	2	356.2
CN014	2019-09-01	3	120.5
CN015	2019-09-01	1	53.23
CN016	2019-09-01	3	25.6
CN012	2019-09-02	5	785
CN015	2019-09-02	2	23.12
CN016	2019-09-02	3	28.3
CN012	2019-09-03	4	36.9
CN014	2019-09-03	2	23.6
CN016	2019-09-03	4	43.5

First, let's load the sample data into DataFrames.

```
import pandas as pd

url_credit='https://raw.githubusercontent.com/billbai0102/Pandas-
Book/master/credit.csv'
url_cards='https://raw.githubusercontent.com/billbai0102/Pandas-
Book/master/cards.csv'
url_trans='https://raw.githubusercontent.com/billbai0102/Pandas-
Book/master/transactions.csv'

df_credit=pd.read_csv(url_credit, parse_dates = ['Approval Date'])
df_cards=pd.read_csv(url_cards, parse_dates = ['Effective Date'])
df_transactions=pd.read_csv(url_trans, parse_dates = ['Date'])
```

3.1 Describing a DataFrame

Once you have a dataset at hand, the first step you want to take is to grasp the bigger picture of your data by describing it. This includes the size of the data, the columns' names and data types, and the basic statistics of each numeric column. Using the DataFrame df_credit as as an example, you can see how to get the bigger picture by describing it.

shape

To get the size of a DataFrame in the format of a tuple (rows, columns), you can access its *shape* attribute.

df_credit.shape

out:

(5, 7)

info()

This function returns a concise summary of the DataFrame, including its indices, each of its columns' names and data types, how many missing value are present in each column, and the DataFrame's overall memory usage. In the result shown below, you can see that there is 1 missing value in the column "Approval Date".

df_credit.info()

out:

```
<class 'pandas.core.frame.DataFrame'>
RangeIndex: 5 entries, 0 to 4
Data columns (total 7 columns):
First Name        5 non-null object
Last Name         5 non-null object
Credit Score      5 non-null int64
Credit Approval   5 non-null bool
Card Name         5 non-null category
Income            5 non-null float64
```

```
Approval Date        4 non-null datetime64[ns]
dtypes: bool(1), category(1), datetime64[ns](1), float64
(1), int64(1), object(2)
memory usage: 530.0+ bytes
```

head()

This function will return the first *n* rows of the DataFrame, with the default being 5. You should leverage this function to get a quick view of the DataFrame, which will allow you to gain basic insights. For example, you may use this function to check whether each columns' data types match your requirements – a scenario you will often be placed in when analyzing and manipulating data.

```
df_credit.head(3)
```

out:

	First Name	Last Name	Credit Score	Credit Approval	Card Name	Income	Approval Date
0	Jacky	White	825	True	Infinite	155000.62	2019-09-13 12:00:00
1	Jane	Nize	812	True	Golden	120800.88	2019-08-16 05:25:00
2	Henry	Tone	780	True	Golden	98000.58	2020-05-06 12:00:00

describe()

Describe() is used to view the basic statistical details of a numerical Series or DataFrame column, such as its median, mean, or percentile statistics. The example below shows how to use *describe()* to get the 68th and 95th percentile values of the DataFrame's columns. Both columns, "Credit Score" and "Income", in df_credit are of a numerical data type, thus their statistics are shown as the result of the *describe()* function.

```
df_credit.describe(percentiles = [.68, .95] )
```

out:

	Credit Score	Income
count	5.00000	5.000000
mean	757.00000	92560.416000
std	81.82298	48800.628682
min	620.00000	35000.000000
50%	780.00000	98000.580000
68%	801.60000	114416.796000
95%	822.00000	148160.672000
max	825.00000	15000.620000

3.2 Indexing DataFrame

Index is the basic object storing axis label for all Pandas objects. In a Series or DataFrame, it serves as an address or row label of the record, which is how any data point across the Series or DataFrame can be accessed. The default index is an integer beginning at **0** and ending at ***length-1*** of the axis. Not only is the index a very convenient way to slice the DataFrame, but it also plays a very import role in merging, pivoting and many more DataFrame manipulation techniques.

index

As the name implies, index is the attribute which shows the index (or row labels) of a DataFrame. The example below shows the default index of df_credit, which is a RangeIndex that ranges between **0** and ***length-1***.

```
df_credit.index
```

out:

```
RangeIndex(start=0, stop=5, step=1)
```

25

set_index()

The *set_index()* function allows you to set the index for a DataFrame using an existing column or list of column names (aka a multiple index).

Setting a single index

```
df_credit.set_index('Card Name', inplace = True)
```

out:

	First Name	Last Name	Credit Score	Credit Approval	Income	Approval Date
Card Name						
Infinite	Jacky	White	825	True	155000.62	2019-09-13
Golden	Jane	Nize	810	True	120800.88	2019-08-16
Golden	Henry	Tone	780	True	98000.58	2020-05-06
Silver	Desmond	Black	750	True	54000.00	2020-05-01
Dividend	Eileen	Musk	620	False	35000.00	NaT

Now that we've changed the DataFrame's index, let's see the new index of df_credit. Notice that the index has now changed to the row label of "Card Name" from the default RangeIndex.

```
df_credit.index
```

out:

```
Index(['Infinite', 'Golden', 'Golden', 'Silver', 'Dividend'],
dtype='object', name='Card Name')
```

Setting a multiple label index

A multiple label index needs a list of column names to work. The example below shows how to set the index of the DataFrame to a combination of "First Name" and "Last Name".

```
df_credit.set_index(['First Name', 'Last Name'], inplace = True)
```

out:

		Credit Score	Credit Approval	Card Name	Income	Approval Date
First Name	**Last Name**					
Jacky	White	825	True	Infinite	155000.62	2019-09-13
Jane	Nize	812	True	Golden	120800.88	2019-08-16
Henry	Tone	780	True	Golden	98000.58	2020-05-06
Desmond	Black	750	True	Silver	54000.00	2020-05-01
Eileen	Musk	620	False	Dividend	35000.00	NaT

Once you set the index using an existing column, you can access the data using the label index. Because the index of df_credit is now set to "First Name" and "Last Name", you can access the first row of df_credit by the label index of "('Jacky', 'White')".

```
df_credit.loc[('Jacky', 'White'), :]
```

out:

```
Credit Score                   825
Credit Approval               True
Card Name                  Infinite
Income                      155001
Approval Date          2019-09-13
Name: (Jacky, White), dtype: object
```

reset_index()

reset_index() allows you to reset the index of a DataFrame to the default integer index beginning at 0. This function is very useful when your operations jumble the index, such as the operations of stacking or slicing the DataFrame, or sorting the DataFrame using a column. The example below shows that after you set the multiple index, *reset_index()* allows you to convert the index back to its default state.

```
df_credit.reset_index(inplace = True)
```

out:

	First Name	Last Name	Credit Score	Credit Approval	Card Name	Income	Approval Date
0	Jacky	White	825	True	Infinite	155000.62	2019-09-13
1	Jane	Nize	812	True	Golden	120800.88	2019-08-16
2	Henry	Tone	780	True	Golden	98000.58	2020-05-06
3	Desmond	Black	750	True	Silver	54000.00	2020-05-01
4	Eileen	Musk	620	False	Dividend	35000.00	NaN

3.3 Slicing Using Index Operator

Pandas allows you to access specific subsets of DataFrames through various methods: using labels (column names), numeric ranges (indices), or specific rows and column index locations. All these access methods need either the indexing operator *[]* or attribute operator *"."* to access to the value of a Series (column) or DataFrame. This means you can access a scalar value of a Series by *Series[label]* or *Series[index]*, or access one column from a DataFrame by *DataFrame[column name]* to return a Series. The index operator *[]* can select multiple columns from the DataFrame at the same time and return a sub DataFrame. For instance, we can select the data of specific columns by using a list [column 1, column 2, ..., column n].

3.3.1 Subset of columns

The examples below show how to use an index operator or attribute operator to access one column from the DataFrame df_credit to return a Series, and how to use the index operator *[]* to get a sub DataFrame by passing a list of multiple column names.

Accessing a single column using the [] operator

```
df_credit['First Name']
```

```
0       Jacky
1        Jane
2       Henry
3     Desmond
4      Eileen
Name: First Name, dtype: object
```

Accessing a single column using the . attributor

```
df_credit.Income
```

out:

```
0     155000.62
1     120800.88
2      98000.58
3      54000.00
4      35000.00
Name: Income, dtype: float64
```

Accessing multiple columns

```
df_credit[['First Name', 'Last Name', 'Credit Approval']]
```

out:

	First Name	Last Name	Credit Score	Credit Approval
0	Jacky	White	825	True
1	Jane	Nize	812	True
2	Henry	Tone	780	True
3	Desmond	Black	750	True
4	Eileen	Musk	620	False

Accessing Series using the index [] operator

Series can also be accessed using the index operator *[]*, which returns a scalar value if a single index is passed, and returns a sub Series if a list of indices is passed.

```
s=df_credit['First Name']
s[1]
```

out:

```
'Jane'
```

The index operator *[]* of a Series returns a sub Series if a list of indices is passed.

```
s[[0,1]]
```

out:

```
0     Jacky
1     Jane
Name: First Name, dtype: object
```

3.3.2 Subset of Rows

Pandas uses the index operator [] to subset rows of a DataFrame. To slice out a subset of rows, use the following syntax: ***DataFrame[start:stop]***, where *start* and *stop* are the default index of the DataFrame. Just like lists in Python, the row at index *start* will be the first included row, and the row at index *stop-1* will be the last row to be included in the subset. If a number isn't specified for *start*, all items from *0* to *stop-1* will be selected. If a number isn't specified for *stop*, all items from *start* to the last item in the DataFrame will be selected. As well, if you input a negative number for *start* or *stop*, and inverse sequence stating from the end is selected, just like lists in Python.

Subsets of rows

To obtain a subset which includes the rows 2 to 4 of a DataFrame, it would look like this:

```
df_credit[2:5]
```

out:

	Credit Score	First Name	Last Name	Credit Approval	Card Name	Income	Approval Date
2	780	Henry	Tone	True	Golden	98000.58	2020-05-06 12:00:00
3	750	Desmond	Black	True	Silver	54000.00	2020-05-01 01:00:00
4	620	Eileen	Musk	False	Dividend	35000.00	NaT

Rows subset using a negative start value

To obtain a subset which includes the first three rows, it would look like this:

```
df_credit[-2:]
```

out:

	First Name	Last Name	Credit Score	Credit Approval	Card Name	Income	Approval Date
0	Jacky	White	825	True	Infinite	155000.62	2019-09-13 12:00:00
1	Jane	Nize	812	True	Golden	120800.88	2019-08-16 05:25:00
2	Henry	Tone	780	True	Golden	98000.58	2020-05-06 12:00:00

Row subset using a negative stop value

To obtain a subset which includes the last two rows, it would look like this:

```
df_credit[:-2]
```

out:

	Credit Score	First Name	Last Name	Credit Approval	Card Name	Income	Approval Date
3	750	Desmond	Black	True	Silver	54000.00	2020-05-01 01:00:00
4	620	Eileen	Musk	False	Dividend	35000.00	NaT

3.4 Slicing Using loc, iloc and ix

Pandas provides the properties *loc[]*, *iloc[]* and *ix[]* to select specific subsets of particular rows and columns from DataFrames. These properties work in either direction of the row or column, and use label and integer-based indexing (positional index).

- *loc* primarily uses label-based indexing.
- *iloc* primarily uses integer-based indexing (positional index).
- *ix* uses a hybrid approach (now deprecated in Pandas 0.20.1)

loc (label-based selection) syntax:

The loc property uses index labels and column names to access data.

> DataFrame.loc[<row >, <column >]
> rows can be:
>   . index/label values, *e.g.,* 'Card Name'
>   . list of label values, *e.g.,* ['First Name', 'Last Name']
>   . logic values, *e.g.,* ['First Name'=='Jane']
>
> columns can be:
>   . index/label values, *e.g.,* 'Card Name'
>   . list of column values, *e.g.,* ['First Name', 'Last Name']
>   . slice of columns values, *e.g.,* ['First Name': Card Name']

Slicing using row index labels

The example below shows how to slice a DataFrame using row index labels.

The output returns a sub DataFrame where the row's index label is 'Golden'

```
df_credit.set_index( 'Card Name', inplace = True)
df_credit.loc['Golden',:]
```

out:

Card Name	Credit Score	First Name	Last Name	Credit Approval	Income	Approval Date
Golden	812	Jane	Nize	True	120800.88	2019-08-16 05:25:00
Golden	780	Henry	Tone	True	98000.58	2020-05-06 12:00:00

Slicing using a list of column names

The example below shows how to slice a DataFrame using a list of column names. The output returns a sub DataFrame with the four columns listed, where the rows' index label is 'Golden'

```
df_credit.loc['Golden',['First Name', 'Last Name', 'Income', 'Approval Date']]
```

out:

Card Name	First Name	Last Name	Income	Approval Date
Golden	Jane	Nize	120800.88	2019-08-16 05:25:00
Golden	Henry	Tone	98000.58	2020-05-06 12:00:00

iloc (position-based selection) syntax:

The *iloc[]* property uses the index position of both rows and columns, and works just like the index operator *[]* to slice a DataFrame.

```
DataFrame.iloc[<row >, <column >]
  rows can be:
  . single row indices, e.g., 1
  . integer list of rows, e.g., [0,1,2]
  . slice of row values, e.g., [0:3]

  columns can be:
  . single column indices, e.g., 2
  . integer list of columns, e.g., [0,1,2]
  . slice of columns indices, e.g., [1:4]
```

Obtaining cell values using position indices

iloc[2,2] returns the cell at the third row and third column of the DataFrame.

```
df_credit.iloc[2,2]
```

out:
```
'780'
```

Slicing using a list of position indices

The example below will return a sub DataFrame with values in the first and third rows, and the first, second, and third columns.

```
df_credit.iloc[[0,2],[0,1,2]]
```

out:

	First Name	Last Name	Credit Score
0	Jacky	White	825
2	Henry	Tone	780

Slicing using a range of position indices

The example below will return a sub DataFrame with values in the first to second row, and first to fourth columns.

```
df_credit.iloc[0:2,0:4]
```

out:

	First Name	Last Name	Credit Score	Credit Approval
0	Jacky	White	825	True
1	Jane	Nize	812	True

Slicing using a range of position indices to get all rows/columns

If no start and stop indices are specified for the row/column indices, the output will return all rows/columns.

```
df_credit.iloc[0:2,:]
```

out:

	Card Name	Credit Score	First Name	Last Name	Credit Approval	Income	Approval Date
0	Infinite	825	Jacky	White	True	155000.62	2019-09-13
1	Golden	812	Jane	Nize	True	120800.88	2019-08-16

3.5 Slicing Using Query Criteria

Pandas offers a flexible and useful slicing method which uses query criteria, and works like the SQL query 'SELECT'. You can slice a DataFrame using logic operators according to your requirements. The logic operators for the query criteria of Pandas are as follows:

Operator	Description
==	Equals
!=	Not equals
> or <	Greater than, less than
>=	Greater than or equal to
<=	Less than or equal to
isin()	To find all that values which contain particular species.
~	The logic "not", the OPPOSITE of the selection that you specify.
&	The logic "and" operator
|	The logic "or" operator
isnull()	Boolean. True if the contents are null.
notnull()	Boolean. True if the contents are not null.

The following examples will show you how to use query criteria to slice DataFrames. Note that query criteria can only be applied to Series (columns), thus, you will need to use DataFrame[column_name] in the query criteria for the logic operation.

Criteria of 'Card Name' equals 'Golden'

```
df_credit.loc[df_credit['Card Name']=='Golden']
```

out:

	Card Name	Credit Score	First Name	Last Name	Credit Approval	Income	Approval Date
1	Golden	810	Jane	Nize	True	120800.88	2019-08-16 05:25:00
2	Golden	780	Henry	Tone	True	98000.58	2020-05-06 12:00:00

Criteria of 'Card Name' does not equal 'Golden'

```
df_credit.loc[~(df_credit['Card Name']=='Golden')]
```

out:

	Card Name	Credit Score	First Name	Last Name	Credit Approval	Income	Approval Date
0	Infinite	825	Jacky	White	True	155000.82	2019-09-13 12:00:00
3	Silver	750	Desmond	Black	True	54000.00	2020-05-01 01:00:00
4	Dividend	620	Eileen	Musk	False	35000.00	NaT

Criteria combination

df_credit.loc[(df_credit['Card Name']=='Golden') & (df_credit['Credit Score']>700)]

out:

	Card Name	Credit Score	First Name	Last Name	Credit Approval	Income	Approval Date
1	Golden	810	Jane	Nize	True	120800.88	2019-08-16 05:25:00
2	Golden	780	Henry	Tone	True	98000.58	2020-05-06 12:00:00

Criteria for column subsets

df_credit.loc[df_credit['Card Name']=='Golden', ['First Name','Last Name']]

out:

	First Name	Last Name
1	Jane	Nize
2	Henry	Tone

Criteria of missing values in a column

df_credit.loc[df_credit['Approval Date'].isnull()]

out:

	First Name	Last Name	Credit Score	Credit Approval	Card Name	Income	Approval Date
4	Eileen	Musk	620	False	Dividend	35000.00	NaT

3.6 Slicing Using any() or all() Functions

Pandas provides the *any()* function to check whether *any* element is True over an axis, and the *all()* function to check whether *all* elements are True over an axis. If the axis is set to 0, the function will check rows, and if set to 1, it will check columns.

In the example below, the axis parameter is set to 1 (column), and returns True if a row contains a NaN value.

```
pd.isnull(df_credit).any(axis=1)
```

out:

```
0      False
1      False
2      False
3      False
4       True
dtype: bool
```

In this second example, the axis parameter is set to 0 (row), and returns True if any column contains a NaN value.

```
pd.isnull(df_credit).any(axis=0)
```

out:

```
First Name        False
Last Name         False
Credit Score      False
Credit Approval   False
Card Name         False
Income            False
Approval Date      True
dtype: bool
```

The examples below exemplify the *any()* and *all()* functions to select row subsets with or without NaN values by first applying the *any()* and *all()*

functions on the DataFrame to get the row index, then using the index operator [] to get the subset of rows.

Select all rows with NaN values using any()

```
df_credit[pd.isnull(df_credit).any(axis=1)]
```

out:

	Card Name	Credit Score	First Name	Last Name	Credit Approval	Income	Approval Date
4	Dividend	620	Eileen	Musk	False	35000.00	NaT

Select all rows without NaN values using all()

```
df_credit[pd.notnull(df_credit).all(axis=1)]
```

out:

	First Name	Last Name	Credit Score	Credit Approval	Card Name	Income	Approval Date
0	Jacky	White	825	True	Infinite	155000.62	2019-09-13
1	Jane	Nize	812	True	Golden	120800.88	2019-08-16
2	Henry	Tone	780	True	Golden	98000.58	2020-05-06
3	Desmond	Black	750	True	Silver	54000.00	2020-05-01

3.7 Sorting DataFrames

Sorting a dataset is a very basic operation in data analysis. Pandas provides the *sort_values()* function to sort rows or columns in a DataFrame based on values of single or multiple columns in ascending or descending order.

sort_values(by, axis, ascending, inplace, kind, na_position, ignore_index)

Arguments:
    by: A string or list of strings of either column names or index labels
       based on which will be sorted.
    axis: (Default is 0) {0: column name; 1: row index labels}
    ascending: (Default is True) {True: ascending; False, descending}

Sorting a DataFrame in ascending order

sort_values() sorts in ascending order by default. In the example below, df_credit is sorted in ascending order by the value of "Income".

```
df_credit.sort_values('Income')
```

out:

	Card Name	Credit Score	First Name	Last Name	Credit Approval	Income	Approval Date	Segment
4	Dividend	620	Eileen	Musk	False	35000.00	NaT	Poor
3	Silver	750	Desmond	Black	True	54000.00	2020-05-01 01:00:00	NaN
2	Golden	780	Henry	Tone	True	98000.58	2020-05-06 12:00:00	Advanced
1	Golden	812	Jane	Nize	True	120800.88	2019-08-16 05:25:00	Excellent
0	Infinite	825	Jacky	White	True	155000.62	2019-09-13 12:00:00	Excellent

Sorting a DataFrame in descending order

If you want to sort a DataFrame in descending order, you'll need to set the option of *ascending* to False. In the example below, df_credit is sorted in descending order by the value of "Income".

```
df_credit.sort_values('Income', ascending = False)
```

out:

	Card Name	Credit Score	First Name	Last Name	Credit Approval	Income	Approval Date	Segment
0	Infinite	825	Jacky	White	True	155000.62	2019-09-13 12:00:00	Excellent
1	Golden	812	Jane	Nize	True	120800.88	2019-08-16 05:25:00	Excellent
2	Golden	780	Henry	Tone	True	98000.58	2020-05-06 12:00:00	Advanced
3	Silver	750	Desmond	Black	True	54000.00	2020-05-01 01:00:00	NaN
4	Dividend	620	Eileen	Musk	False	35000.00	NaT	Poor

Sorting a DataFrame by multiple columns

Frequently, you will encounter problems where you'll need to sort a DataFrame by multiple columns, and in different orders for each column. Luckily, the sort_values() function is capable of doing so if you provide a list of column names to the *by* parameter, and a list of booleans to the ***ascending*** parameter, in which the order of the boolean list corresponds to the order of the column name list.

The example below shows how to sort df_credit in ascending order for "Credit Score" and descending order for "Income".

```
df_credit.sort_values(['Credit Score', 'Income'] ,ascending = [True, False])
```

out:

	Card Name	Credit Score	First Name	Last Name	Credit Approval	Income	Approval Date	Segment
4	Dividend	620	Eileen	Musk	False	35000.00	NaT	Poor
3	Silver	750	Desmond	Black	True	54000.00	2020-05-01 01:00:00	NaN
2	Golden	780	Henry	Tone	True	98000.58	2020-05-06 12:00:00	Advanced
1	Golden	812	Jane	Nize	True	120800.88	2019-08-16 05:25:00	Excellent
0	Infinite	825	Jacky	White	True	155000.62	2019-09-13 12:00:00	Excellent

Chapter 4   Modifying DataFrames

In most real-life scenarios, you'll often find yourself in a place where you'll need to make changes to an existing DataFrame before further analysis. This chapter introduces how to modify a DataFrame such as adding data, deleting data, and replacing cell contents of a DataFrame. Additionally, this chapter introduces the functions which process DataFrame datatypes such as string, math, and datetime.

4.1 Adding New Columns

It is very common to add new columns to an existing DataFrame without changing any preexisting data. You can add new columns to a DataFrame using the indexing operator "*[]*" or *assign()* function.

Adding new columns using the [] operator

The instance below will add a new column "Audited" with every row defaulted to the Boolean 'True'.

```
df_credit['Audited'] = True
```

out:

	First Name	Last Name	Credit Score	Credit Approval	Card Name	Income	Approval Date	Audited
0	Jacky	White	825	True	Infinite	155000.62	2019-09-13	True
1	Jane	Nize	812	True	Golden	120800.88	2019-08-16	True
2	Henry	Tone	780	True	Golden	98000.58	2020-05-06	True
3	Desmond	Black	750	True	Silver	54000.00	2020-05-01	True
4	Eileen	Musk	620	False	Dividend	35000.00	NaT	True

Adding new columns by deriving values from existing columns

The example below creates a new column "Full Name", by combining the existing columns "First Name" and "Last Name".

```
df_credit['Full Name'] = df_credit['First Name'] + ' ' + df_credit['Last Name']
```

out:

	First Name	Last Name	Credit Score	Credit Approval	Card Name	Income	Approval Date	Full Name
0	Jacky	White	825	True	Infinite	155000.62	2019-09-13	Jacky White
1	Jane	Nize	812	True	Golden	120800.88	2019-08-16	Jane Nize
2	Henry	Tone	780	True	Golden	98000.58	2020-05-06	Henry Tone
3	Desmond	Black	750	True	Silver	54000.00	2020-05-01	Desmond Black
4	Eileen	Musk	620	False	Dividend	35000.00	NaT	Eileen Musk

Adding new columns using the assign() function

The *assign()* function not only adds new columns to a DataFrame, but can also create a new copy of the DataFrame with requested changes, while keeping the original DataFrame untouched.

```
df = df_credit.assign(Full_Name = df_credit['Last Name'] + ', ' + df_credit['First Name'] )
```

out:

	First Name	Last Name	Credit Score	Credit Approval	Card Name	Income	Approval Date	Full_Name
0	Jacky	White	825	True	Infinite	155000.62	2019-09-13	White, Jacky
1	Jane	Nize	812	True	Golden	120800.88	2019-08-16	Nize, Jane
2	Henry	Tone	780	True	Golden	98000.58	2020-05-06	Tone, Henry
3	Desmond	Black	750	True	Silver	54000.00	2020-05-01	Black, Desmond
4	Eileen	Musk	620	False	Dividend	35000.00	NaT	Musk, Eileen

Renaming columns

Renaming existing columns can be done using the *rename()* function, by passing a dict-like parameter "{'old column name': 'new column name'}" to the option "columns". The example below demonstrates how to rename the columns "First Name" and "Last Name" to "First" and "Last" in df_credit.

```
df_credit.rename(columns={'First Name':'First', 'Last Name': 'Last'},inplace =
True)
```

out:

	First	Last	Credit Score	Credit Approval	Card Name	Income	Approval Date
0	Jacky	White	825	True	Infinite	155000.62	2019-09-13
1	Jane	Nize	812	True	Golden	120800.88	2019-08-16
2	Henry	Tone	780	True	Golden	98000.58	2020-05-06
3	Desmond	Black	750	True	Silver	54000.00	2020-05-01
4	Eileen	Musk	620	False	Dividend	35000.00	NaT

4.2 Adding New Rows

You can add new rows to a DataFrame using the *append()* function, or the index operators, *loc[]* and *iloc[]*. The *loc[]* operator works on label-based indices, meaning you'll need to specify the label indices of the rows you are adding, and the *iloc[]* operator works on index-based indices meaning you'll need to specify the integer indices of the new rows.

Adding new rows using append()

The *append()* function works by adding new rows to a DataFrame, given a dictionary with the same structure as the targeted DataFrame. Note that *append()* is immutable, thus, it does not change the existing DataFrame itself, but returns a new DataFrame with the new row appended.

43

```
append(other, ignore_index, verify_integrity)
```

Arguments :
    other: DataFrame or Series/dict-like object to append
    ignore_index: boolean, must be set to True

```
df_credit = df_credit.append({'First Name': 'John', 'Last Name': 'Abuli','Credit Score':785}, ignore_index=True)
```

out:

	First Name	Last Name	Credit Score	Credit Approval	Card Name	Income	Approval Date
0	Jacky	White	825	True	Infinite	155000.62	2019-09-13
1	Jane	Nize	812	True	Golden	120800.88	2019-08-16
2	Henry	Tone	780	True	Golden	98000.58	2020-05-06
3	Desmond	Black	750	True	Silver	54000.00	2020-05-01
4	Eileen	Musk	620	False	Dividend	35000.00	NaT
5	John	Abuli	785	NaN	NaN	NaN	NaT

Adding new rows using loc[]

Adding new rows using *loc[]* requires a list which includes the new rows'
contents. If the DataFrame already has any rows with the same index name, it
will replace the row with the new content.

```
df_credit = df_credit.set_index('Credit Score')
df_credit.loc[685] = ['Johnny', 'Haw','','','','' ]
```

out:

Credit Score	First Name	Last Name	Credit Approval	Card Name	Income	Approval Date
825	Jacky	White	True	Infinite	155000.62	2019-09-13
810	Jane	Nize	True	Golden	120800.88	2019-08-16
780	Henry	Tone	True	Golden	98000.6	2020-05-06
750	Desmond	Black	True	Silver	54000.00	2020-05-01
620	Eileen	Musk	False	Dividend	35000.00	NaT
685	Johnny	Haw				

Adding new rows using iloc[]

As mentioned previously, the *iloc* property works on index positions. Thus, if you need to add a new row to a specific index position, you may use *iloc*. Just like the *loc* operator, *iloc[]* will replace an existing row's contents if the specified index position already exists. As seen below, the third row is replaced with the new data since the specified index position already exists in the DataFrame.

```
df_credit.iloc[2] = ['Johnny', 'Haw','','','','',' ' ]
```

out:

	First Name	Last Name	Credit Score	Credit Approval	Card Name	Income	Approval Date
0	Jacky	White	825	True	Infinite	155000.62	2019-09-13
1	Jane	Nize	812	True	Golden	120800.88	2019-08-16
2	Johnny	Haw					
3	Desmond	Black	750	True	Silver	54000.00	2020-05-01
4	Eileen	Musk	620	False	Dividend	35000.00	NaT

4.3 Dropping Rows or Columns

If any rows or columns of a DataFrame are not of use any more, they can be removed to reduce the size of a DataFrame and improve efficiency. To do this, Pandas provides the *drop()* function to remove rows or columns out of a DataFrame, by specifying an axis and a corresponding list of labels or indices. If you need to drop data and overwrite the current DataFrame, you may set the *inplace* parameter to True.

```
drop(self, labels, axis, index, columns, level, inplace, errors)
```

Arguments:
    labels: single label or list, Index or column labels to drop.
    axis: 0 or 'index', drop rows by the labels from index (default)
             1 or 'columns', drop columns by column names

Dropping rows by index position

To drop rows by index position, all you need to pass is a list of index positions to the function, since rows is the default axis of the *drop()* function. The example below shows how to drop the 1st and 4th rows.

```
df_credit.drop([0, 3])
```

out:

	First Name	Last Name	Credit Score	Credit Approval	Card Name	Income	Approval Date
1	Jane	Nize	812	True	Golden	120800.88	2019-08-16
2	Henry	Tone	780	True	Golden	98000.58	2020-05-06
4	Eileen	Musk	620	False	Dividend	35000.00	NaT

Dropping rows by index label

If the index of a row is an index label, you can drop the rows with a list of row index labels. The example below shows how to drop the rows with an index label of "Jane" and "Eileen".

```
df_credit = df_credit.set_index('First Name')
df_credit.drop(['Jane', 'Eileen'])
```

out:

First Name	Last Name	Credit Score	Credit Approval	Card Name	Income	Approval Date
Jacky	White	825	True	Infinite	155000.62	2019-09-13
Henry	Tone	780	True	Golden	98000.58	2020-05-06
Desmond	Black	750	True	Silver	54000.00	2020-05-01

Dropping rows by conditions on column values

If you want to drop rows by using conditions on the columns, you can pass a list indices of the rows satisfying the dropping conditions to the *drop()* function. The indices can be found through the *index* attribute of the sub DataFrame. The example below drops all rows where the value of "Credit Score" is less than 780 or "Credit Approval" is False.

```
row_index = df_credit[(df_credit['Credit Approval'] == False)|(df_credit['Credit Score']<780)].index

df_credit.drop(row_index)
```

out:

	First Name	Last Name	Credit Score	Credit Approval	Card Name	Income	Approval Date
0	Jacky	White	825	True	Infinite	155000.62	2019-09-13
1	Jane	Nize	812	True	Golden	120800.88	2019-08-16
2	Henry	Tone	780	True	Golden	98000.58	2020-05-06

Dropping columns by column names

To drop columns by their names, you must pass a list of column names to the *drop()* function and set *axis* to 1. The example below drops the columns "Credit Approval" and "Card Name".

```
df_credit.drop(['Credit Approval', 'Card Name'], axis = 1)
```

out:

	First Name	Last Name	Credit Score	Income	Approval Date
0	Jacky	White	825	155000.62	2019-09-13
1	Jane	Nize	812	120800.88	2019-08-16
2	Henry	Tone	780	98000.58	2020-05-06
3	Desmond	Black	750	54000.00	2020-05-01
4	Eileen	Musk	620	35000.00	NaT

Dropping columns by index position

If column names aren't present in a DataFrame, you may use the columns' index positions to drop them. Here is an example to drop the 3rd and 4th columns.

```
df_credit.drop([df_credit.columns[2], df_credit.columns[3]], axis = 1)
```

out:

	First Name	Last Name	Card Name	Income	Approval Date
0	Jacky	White	Infinite	155000.62	2019-09-13
1	Jane	Nize	Golden	120800.88	2019-08-16
2	Henry	Tone	Golden	98000.58	2020-05-06
3	Desmond	Black	Silver	54000.00	2020-05-01
4	Eileen	Musk	Dividend	35000.00	NaT

4.4 Modifying DataFrame

As a data scientist, you'll often need to modify specific values in a DataFrame before further processing or analysis. These values may be a subset or particular cells of a DataFrame. As previously discussed, *loc[], iloc[] and ix[]* can slice a DataFrame to requested subsets based on the DataFrame's labels, indices or a mix of both. With the same concept, they can also be used to change the values of a specific subset as they slice the DataFrame.

loc[]

The *loc[]* operator is label based, meaning it uses index labels or Boolean indices from query criteria to modify the values of a specific cell or sub DataFrame.

```
loc[<row >, <column >] = <new value>
```

In the example below you'll see that a new column "Segment" is created in df_credit, and its values are modified to different values according to different Boolean conditions.

Creating a new column and setting values conditionally

The column "Segment" is created, and its values are set to "Excellent" if "Credit Score" > 800.

```
df_credit.loc[df_credit['Credit Score'] > 800, 'Segment' ] = 'Excellent'
```

out:

	Card Name	Credit Score	First Name	Last Name	Credit Approval	Income	Approval Date	Segment
0	Infinite	825	Jacky	White	True	155000.62	2019-09-13 12:00:00	Excellent
1	Golden	812	Jane	Nize	True	120800.88	2019-08-16 05:25:00	Excellent
2	Golden	780	Henry	Tone	True	98000.58	2020-05-06 12:00:00	NaN
3	Silver	750	Desmond	Black	True	54000.00	2020-05-01 01:00:00	NaN
4	Dividend	620	Eileen	Musk	False	35000.00	NaT	NaN

Modifying column values conditionally

The values in the column "Segment" are modified to "Poor" if "Credit Score < 700"

```
df_credit.loc[df_credit['Credit Score'] < 700, 'Segment' ] = 'Poor'
```

out:

	Card Name	Credit Score	First Name	Last Name	Credit Approval	Income	Approval Date	Segment
0	Infinite	825	Jacky	White	True	155000.62	2019-09-13 12:00:00	Excellent
1	Golden	812	Jane	Nize	True	120800.88	2019-08-16 05:25:00	Excellent
2	Golden	780	Henry	Tone	True	98000.58	2020-05-06 12:00:00	NaN
3	Silver	750	Desmond	Black	True	54000.00	2020-05-01 01:00:00	NaN
4	Dividend	620	Eileen	Musk	False	35000.00	NaT	Poor

"Segment" values are modified to "Advanced" if Credit Score is less than or equal to 800 and "Income" is greater than 80000

49

```
df_credit.loc[(df_credit['Credit Score'] <= 800) & (df_credit['Income']> 80000),
'Segment' ] = 'Advanced'
```

out:

	Card Name	Credit Score	First Name	Last Name	Credit Approval	Income	Approval Date	Segment
0	Infinite	825	Jacky	White	True	155000.62	2019-09-13 12:00:00	Excellent
1	Golden	812	Jane	Nize	True	120800.88	2019-08-16 05:25:00	Excellent
2	Golden	780	Henry	Tone	True	98000.58	2020-05-06 12:00:00	Advanced
3	Silver	750	Desmond	Black	True	54000.00	2020-05-01 01:00:00	NaN
4	Dividend	620	Eileen	Musk	False	35000.00	NaT	Poor

iloc[]

```
iloc[<row >, <column >] = new value
```

The syntax of *iloc[]* is fundamentally the same as *loc[]*, except it works on position-based indices instead. The example below shows how to access and modify the cell value in the fifth row and fourth column of the DataFrame.

Accessing the cell value using iloc

```
df_credit.iloc[4,3]
```

out:

```
False
```

Modifying the cell value from "False" to "True" using iloc

```
df_credit.iloc[4,3] = True
```

out:

	First Name	Last Name	Credit Score	Credit Approval	Card Name	Income	Approval Date
0	Jacky	White	825	True	Infinite	155000.62	2019-09-13
1	Jane	Nize	812	True	Golden	120800.88	2019-08-16
2	Henry	Tone	780	True	Golden	98000.58	2020-05-06
3	Desmond	Black	750	True	Silver	54000.00	2020-05-01
4	Eileen	Musk	620	True	Dividend	35000.00	NaT

ix[]

ix[<row >, <column >] = new value

The *ix[]* operator works on hybrid indices. The example below shows how to modify a cell value based on row position and column name.

Accessing the cell value using ix[]

This example below passes the arguments [4,'Approval Date'] to the ix operator to get the cell value of the 5th row and column "Approval Date".

df_credit.ix[4,'Approval Date']

out:

nan

Modifying the cell value from "NaN" to "2020-06-20" by ix

df_credit.ix[4,'Approval Date'] = '2020-06-20'

out:

	First Name	Last Name	Credit Score	Credit Approval	Card Name	Income	Approval Date
0	Jacky	White	825	True	Infinite	155000.62	2019-09-13
1	Jane	Nize	812	True	Golden	120800.88	2019-08-16
2	Henry	Tone	780	True	Golden	98000.58	2020-05-06
3	Desmond	Black	750	True	Silver	54000.00	2020-05-01
4	Eileen	Musk	620	True	Dividend	35000.00	2020-06-20

51

mask()

Pandas provides the *mask()* function to modify an entire Series or DataFrame according to an if-then condition. Its two parameters, "cond" and "other", accomplishes this exactly. It iterates over each cell value in each cell, and if "cond" is False then the original cell value is kept; otherwise the corresponding cell value is replaced by the value passed to "other". The *mask()* function is very useful when you need to replace the values of a DataFrame conditionally.

mask(self, cond, other, inplace, axis, level, errors, try_cast)

Arguments:
    cond: boolean condition. replace the cell value if True, keep if False
    other: the value that will be used to replace the cell if cond is False

Using mask() on columns

The example below shows how to use *mask()* on the column "Income". If "Income" is greater than 100,000 then the value is replaced with 100,000. Otherwise, the original value is kept.

```
df_credit['Income'] = df_credit['Income'].mask( df_credit['Income'] > 100000,
100000 )
```

out:

	First Name	Last Name	Credit Score	Credit Approval	Card Name	Income	Approval Date
0	Jacky	White	825	True	Infinite	100000.00	2019-09-13
1	Jane	Nize	812	True	Golden	100000.00	2019-08-16
2	Henry	Tone	780	True	Golden	98000.58	2020-05-06
3	Desmond	Black	750	True	Silver	54000.00	2020-05-01
4	Eileen	Musk	620	True	Dividend	35000.00	NaT

Using mask() on a DataFrame

The example below shows how to use *mask()* on an entire DataFrame. In the particular example, if any cell value in df_credit is missing, then it is replaced with "Not Approved". Otherwise, the original value is kept.

```
df_credit.mask( df_credit.isna(),'Not Approved' )
```

out:

	First Name	Last Name	Credit Score	Credit Approval	Card Name	Income	Approval Date
0	Jacky	White	825	True	Infinite	155000.62	2019-09-13
1	Jane	Nize	812	True	Golden	120800.88	2019-08-16
2	Henry	Tone	780	True	Golden	98000.58	2020-05-06
3	Desmond	Black	750	True	Silver	54000.00	2020-05-01
4	Eileen	Musk	620	True	Dividend	35000.00	Not Approved

4.5 Mathematical Functions

In the previous parts, you've been introduced to modifying DataFrames through adding and dropping values, and modifying specific values of rows and columns with a new set value. However, in the real world, the new modified value of a cell is often derived from running mathematical calculations or performing operations on values from other rows and columns. Luckily for you, Pandas has many built-in functions to help you accomplish this. This section will teach you how to apply mathematical calculation functions on a DataFrame. String operations and datetime processing functions will be introduced in next section.

Since Pandas is built on NumPy, NumPy's universal functions (ufuncs) works element by element on Pandas' Series and DataFrame objects. This is called vectorized operations. For unary operations, the ufuncs preserve index

53

and column labels in the output; And for binary operations, Pandas will automatically align indices when passing the objects to the ufunc.

Pandas also provides a set of math operators such as addition and subtraction which make it easy to perform mathematical calculations on your DataFrame. Please note that these functions and operators ignore missing/NaN values. That means, the results of all mathematical operations on NaN will be NaN as well. Here are some examples of using basic mathematical operations on DataFrames.

Basic mathematical operations

In the example below, the DataFrame df_credit applies the basic math operations of addition, subtraction, multiplication, and division on its numerical column "Income". In this example, the value of cell [4,5] is intentionally set to NaN to show the results of math operations on NaN values.

```
df_credit.ix[4,5]=np.nan
df_credit['Plus_1000'] = df_credit['Income'] + 1000
df_credit['Minus_1000'] = df_credit['Income'] - 1000
df_credit['Mutiply_10'] = df_credit['Income'] * 10
df_credit['Divid_10'] = df_credit['Income'] / 10
df_credit['Income_to_Credit'] = df_credit['Income'] / df_credit['Credit Score']
```

out:

	First Name	Last Name	Credit Score	...	Plus_1000	Minus_1000	Mutiply_10	Divid_10	Income_to_credit
0	Jacky	White	825	...	156000.62	154000.62	1550006.2	15500.062	187.879539
1	Jane	Nize	812	...	121800.88	119800.88	1208008.8	12080.088	149.136889
2	Henry	Tone	780	...	99000.58	97000.58	980005.8	9800.058	125.641769
3	Desmond	Black	750	...	55000.00	53000.00	540000.0	5400.000	72.000000
4	Eileen	Musk	620	...	NaN	NaN	NaN	NaN	NaN

Applying ufunc functions

If we apply a NumPy ufunc on Pandas objects, the result will be another Pandas object which keeps the same index for unary operations, and aligns indices for multiple objects.

```
import numpy as np
df_credit['log_Income'] = np.log(df_credit['Income'])
```

out:

	First Name	Last Name	Credit Score	Credit Approval	Card Name	Income	Approval Date	log_Income
0	Jacky	White	825	True	Infinite	155000.62	2019-09-13	11.951184
1	Jane	Nize	812	True	Golden	120800.88	2019-08-16	11.701899
2	Henry	Tone	780	True	Golden	98000.58	2020-05-06	11.492729
3	Desmond	Black	750	True	Silver	54000.00	2020-05-01	10.896739
4	Elieen	Musk	620	False	Dividend	35000.00	NaT	10.463103

Pandas provides many useful mathematical functions which are extremely important for numerical data calculations used in data science. Below are said mathematical functions.

NumPy Math Functions

Arithmetic operations	
Function	**Description**
pow(x, y)	Returns x raised to the power y
modf(x)	Returns the fractional and integer parts of x
fmod(x, y)	Returns the remainder when x is divided by y
sqrt(x)	Returns the square root of x
fabs(x)	Returns the absolute value of x

Exponents and logarithms

Function	Description
exp(x)	Returns e**x
expm1(x)	Returns e**x − 1
log(x[, base])	Returns the logarithm of x to the base (defaults to e)
log10(x)	Returns the base-10 logarithm of x

Rounding

Function	Description
floor(x)	Returns the floor x
ceil(x)	Returns the ceiling of x
trunc(x)	Returns the truncated integer value of x

Trigonometric functions

Function	Description
sin(x)	Returns the sine of x
cos(x)	Returns the cosine of x
tan(x)	Returns the tangent of x
asin(x)	Returns the arc sine of x
acos(x)	Returns the arc cosine of x
atan(x)	Returns the arc tangent of x
hypot(x, y)	Returns the Euclidean norm, sqrt(x*x + y*y)

Hyperbolic functions

Function	Description
sinh(x)	Returns the hyperbolic cosine of x
cosh(x)	Returns the hyperbolic cosine of x
tanh(x)	Returns the hyperbolic tangent of x

Floating point routines

Function	Description
frexp(x)	Returns the mantissa and exponent of x as the pair (m, e)

4.6 String Functions

String functions can help you obtain clean and organized textual information from a dataset, by processing words and sentences. This section will introduce basic string operations in Pandas, such as changing cases, finding substrings, finding the length of a string, joining and splitting strings, replacing characters, and much more.

Pandas uses Python's default indexing operator [] to access the items in a string, since it is of a sequence datatype. For example, df_credit['First Name'].str[0:3] gets the first 3 characters of each row of the column "First Name" in df_credit.

Pandas provides a set of vectorized string processing functions for Series and DataFrames. These functions can be called using the *str* attribute and excludes missing/NA values automatically. This means that Pandas will throw an error message if you attempt to apply string functions to missing/NA values. Pandas' string functions generally use the same names as Python's built-in string functions. Additionally, Pandas also provides some functions which use regular expressions to work on matching or processing string patterns. Here are several code examples of using Pandas' string functions.

```
#slicing
df_credit['First_3'] = df_credit['First Name'].str[0:3]

#combining 2 columns
df_credit['Last_First'] = df_credit['Last Name'] + ',' + df_credit['First Name']

#find function
df_credit['First_Find Ja'] = df_credit['First Name'].str.find('Ja')

#  regular expressions match
df_credit['First_Match Ja'] = df_credit['First Name'].str.match('Ja')
```

out:

	First Name	Last Name	...	First_3	Last_First	First_Find Ja	First_Match Ja
0	Jacky	White	...	Jac	White, Jacky	0	True
1	Jane	Nize	...	Jan	Nize, Jane	0	True
2	Henry	Tone	...	Hen	Tone, Henry	-1	False
3	Desmond	Black	...	Des	Black, Desmond	-1	False
4	Eileen	Musk	...	Eil	Musk, Eileen	-1	False

Below are the most important Pandas string functions:

Selected string functions

Function	Describe
len(s)	Length of s
s.count(s2)	Count of s2 in s

Find / Replace

Function	Describe
s2 in s	Return true if s contains s2
s2 not in s	Return true if s does not contain s2
s.index(s2, i, j)	Index of first occurrence of s2 in s after index i and before index j
s.find(s2)	Find and return lowest index of s2 in s
s.index(s2)	Return lowest index of s2 in s (but raise ValueError if not found)

58

s.replace(s2, s3)	Replace s2 with s3 in s
s.rfind(s2)	Return highest index of s2 in s
s.rindex(s2)	Return highest index of s2 in s (raise ValueError if not found)
s.get(i)	Return ith element in s

Concatnation

Function	Describe
s + s2	Concat s and s2
s.join(Series)	Join strings in each element of the Series with passed separator

Substring/Split

Function	Describe
s[i:j]	Substring of s from i to j
s.split(sep)	Return list of s split by sep

Whitespace

Function	Describe
s.strip()	Remove leading and trailing whitespace from s
s.lstrip()	Remove leading whitespace from s
s.rstrip()	Remove trailing whitespace from s

Case

Function	Describe
s.capitalize()	Capitalize s
s.lower()	Lowercase s
s.upper()	Uppercase s
s.islower()	Return true if s is lowercase
s.isupper()	Return true if s is uppercase

Regular expressions	
Function	**Describe**
s.match(re)	Call re.match() on each element, returning a boolean.
s.extract(re)	Call re.match() on each element, returning matched groups as strings.
s.findall(re)	Call re.findall() on each element

4.7 Working with Date and Time

Time series data is a measure of values at different points in time. Usually it has 3 types: timestamps that represent specific times, time intervals that measure periods of time, and time deltas that represent differences in time. This section will introduce the formats of date and time, and how Pandas works with it.

Pandas provides an extensive set of powerful and easy to use functions to work with date and time, since it was originally developed for financial time series data, such as daily stock market prices. Pandas uses the Timestamp object to handle date and time, which is a combination of NumPy's datetime64 datatype and Python's datetime and dateutil modules.

Reading date and time into Pandas

Pandas provides the *to_datetime()* function to create a timestamp (a single time point) from a string, in a wide variety of date and time formats. The example below converts several accepted formats of date and time into a Timestamp object.

```
pd.to_datetime(['2020-06-05', '6/6/2020', 'June 7,2020', '2020-06-15 12:20pm'])
```

out:
```
DatetimeIndex(['2020-06-05 00:00:00', '2020-06-06 00:00:00',
               '2020-06-07 00:00:00', '2020-06-15 12:20:00'],
               dtype='datetime64[ns]', freq=None)
```

If a list of input strings are all in the same date/time format, you can explicitly specify the *format* parameter to greatly speed up the performance of ***to_datetime()***, especially when you're working with a large dataset.

Any data/time format accepted by Python's *strftime()* and *strptime()* functions may be used to specify a Timestamp format. The example below uses the format %d/%m/%y %H:%M:%S %p" to specify the input string format.

```
pd.to_datetime(['6/5/20 12:00:00 PM', '6/6/20 5:25:00 AM', '6/7/20 6:30:00 PM'], format='%d/%m/%y %H:%M:%S %p')
```

out:
```
DatetimeIndex(['2020-05-06 12:00:00', '2020-06-06 05:25:00',
              '2020-07-06 06:30:00'],dtype='datetime64[ns]', freq=None)
```

Since date and time has many formats in the real world, it is very important to know the format conversion functions between string and datetime: *strftime()* converts a datetime object and specified format to a string representing date and time, and *strptime()* creates a datetime object from a string and specified format. Examples of how to use *strptime()* and *strftime()* are shown as below.

```
from datetime import datetime
str_datetime = '06/20/20 13:55:26'

#read datetime from string using strptime
dt_example = datetime.strptime(str_datetime, '%m/%d/%y %H:%M:%S')
print('type of dt_example: ' + str(type(dt_example)))
print(dt_example)

#output datetime to string using strftime
str_example = datetime.strftime(dt_example, '%Y-%m-%d')
print('type of str_example: ' + str(type(str_example)))
print( str_example)
```

out:

```
type of dt_example: <class 'datetime.datetime'>
2020-06-20 13:55:26
type of str_example: <class 'str'>
2020-06-20
```

Since Python calls platform's C strftime() function for its own strftime() function, you should know the strftime() format codes(1989 C Standard), as it applies directly to Python.

strftime() and strptime() Format Codes (1989 c Standard)

Directive	Meaning
%a	Locale's abbreviated weekday name.
%A	Locale's full weekday name.
%b	Locale's abbreviated month name.
%B	Locale's full month name.
%c	Locale's appropriate date and time representation.
%d	Day of the month as a decimal number [01,31].
%f	Microsecond as a decimal number [0,999999], zero-padded on the left
%H	Hour (24-hour clock) as a decimal number [00,23].
%I	Hour (12-hour clock) as a decimal number [01,12].
%j	Day of the year as a decimal number [001,366].
%m	Month as a decimal number [01,12].

%M	Minute as a decimal number [00,59].
%p	Locale's equivalent of either AM or PM.
%S	Second as a decimal number [00,59].
%U	Week number of the year (Sunday as the first day of the week) as a decimal number [00,53]. All days in a new year preceding the first Sunday are considered to be in week 0.
%w	Weekday as a decimal number [0(Sunday),6].
%W	Week number of the year (Monday as the first day of the week) as a decimal number [00,53]. All days in a new year preceding the first Monday are considered to be in week 0.
%x	Locale's appropriate date representation.
%X	Locale's appropriate time representation.
%y	Year without century as a decimal number [00,99].
%Y	Year with century as a decimal number [0001,9999] (strptime), [1000,9999] (strftime).
%z	UTC offset in the form +HHMM or -HHMM (empty string if the the object is naive).
%Z	Time zone name (empty string if the object is naive).
%%	A literal '%' character.

With these versatile format codes, you can convert any datetime object to a date/time string specified by the format you want. Below, the example converts a datetime object to a weekday string by using the format code '%A' (full weekday name format):

```
weekday = pd.to_datetime(['6/5/20', '6/6/20', '6/7/20', np.nan], format="%m/%d/%y')
weekday.strftime('%A')
```

out:
```
Index(['Friday', 'Saturday', 'Sunday', 'NaT'], dtype='object')
```

For DataFrames, you can convert their datetime column values to DatetimeIndex objects, then apply the *strftime()* function to creat formatted strings for new columns. The example below shows how to use the *strftime()* function to get a formatted data/time string from the datetime type column "Approval Date"

```
df_credit['Week Day'] = pd.DatetimeIndex(df_credit['Approval Date']).strftime('%A')

df_credit['Approval Year'] = pd.DatetimeIndex(df_credit['Approval Date']).strftime('%Y')

df_credit['Approval Month'] = pd.DatetimeIndex(df_credit['Approval Date']).strftime('%m')

df_credit['Approval MONTH'] = pd.DatetimeIndex(df_credit['Approval Date']).strftime('%B')

df_credit['Approval Day'] = pd.DatetimeIndex(df_credit['Approval Date']).strftime('%d')
```

out:

	First Name	Last Name	...	Approval Date	Approval Day	Week Day	Approval Year	Approval Month	Approval MONTH
0	Jacky	White	...	2019-09-13 12:00:00	13	Friday	2019	09	September
1	Jane	Nize	...	2019-08-16 05:25:00	16	Friday	2019	08	August
2	Henry	Tone	...	2019-09-13 12:00:00	13	Friday	2019	09	September
3	Desmond	Black	...	2019-08-16 05:25:00	16	Friday	2019	08	August
4	Eileen	Musk	...	NaT	NaT	NaT	NaT	NaT	NaT

Properties of datetime object

Pandas can also use the *dt* attribute to access datetime-like properties of the datetime values. The example below shows how to access the "Approval Date" column using the *dt* attribute to create new columns from its properties, such as day, month, and year. However, the output from the *dt* attribute is index-like, not a string as *strftime()* outputs.

```
df_credit['Year'] = df_credit['Approval Date'].dt.year
df_credit['Month'] = df_credit['Approval Date'].dt.month
df_credit['Day'] = df_credit['Approval Date'].dt.day
df_credit['Week'] = df_credit['Approval Date'].dt.week
```

out:

	First Name	Last Name	...	Approval Date	Year	Month	Day	Week
0	Jacky	White	...	2019-09-13 12:00:00	2019.0	9.0	13.0	37.0
1	Jane	Nize	...	2019-08-16 05:25:00	2019.0	8.0	16.0	33.0
2	Henry	Tone	...	2019-09-13 12:00:00	2019.0	9.0	13.0	37.0
3	Desmond	Black	...	2019-08-16 05:25:00	2019.0	8.0	16.0	33.0
4	Eileen	Musk	...	NaT	NaN	NaN	NaN	NaN

Datetime properties

Property	Description
year	The year of the datetime
month	The month of the datetime
day	The days of the datetime
hour	The hour of the datetime
minute	The minutes of the datetime
second	The seconds of the datetime
microsecond	The microseconds of the datetime
nanosecond	The nanoseconds of the datetime
date	Returns datetime.date (does not contain timezone information)
time	Returns datetime.time (does not contain timezone information)
timetz	Returns datetime.time as local time with timezone information
dayofyear	The ordinal day of year
weekofyear	The week ordinal of the year
week	The week ordinal of the year
dayofweek	The number of the day of the week with Monday=0, Sunday=6
weekday	The number of the day of the week with Monday=0, Sunday=6
quarter	Quarter of the date: Jan-Mar = 1, Apr-Jun = 2, etc.
days_in_month	The number of days in the month of the datetime
is_month_start	Logical indicating if first day of month (defined by frequency)
is_month_end	Logical indicating if last day of month (defined by frequency)
is_quarter_start	Logical indicating if first day of quarter (defined by frequency)
is_quarter_end	Logical indicating if last day of quarter (defined by frequency)
is_year_start	Logical indicating if first day of year (defined by frequency)

65

is_year_end	Logical indicating if last day of year (defined by frequency)
is_leap_year	Logical indicating if the date belongs to a leap year

Working with datetime functions

We've already learned that the *to_datetime()* function creates a timestamp from a string. In addition to this function, Pandas also provides the *to_timedelta()* function to convert an argument to a timedelta (the duration between two datetime objects). Timedeltas may be used for datetime calculations and are complimented by two functions *DateOffset()* which is a date increment used for date ranges, and *date_range()* which creates a fixed frequency DatetimeIndex.

Timedelta()

The example below adds a timedelta of 5 days to the timestamp (2020-06-06)

```
date_ex = pd.Timestamp('2020-06-06')
dt_delta = pd.to_timedelta(5,unit='D')
date_after_delta = date_ex + dt_delta
date_after_delta
```

out:

```
Timestamp('2020-06-11 00:00:00')
```

DateOffset()

The example below adds a DateOffset of 5 days to the timestamp (2020-06-06)

```
pd.Timestamp('2020-06-06') + pd.DateOffset(days=5)
```

out:

```
Timestamp('2020-06-11 00:00:00')
```

The example below uses Python's datetime module to create 3 columns – "Today" which returns the date of today, "Audit" which calculates the duration between "Approval Date" and today, and "Duration" which applies a DateOffset of 3 months to "Approval Date".

```
import datetime as dt
df_credit['Today'] = dt.datetime.today()
df_credit['Audit'] = df_credit['Today'] - df_credit['Approval Date']
df_credit['Duration'] = df_credit['Approval Date'] + pd.DateOffset(months=3)
```

out:

	First Name	Last Name	...	Approval Date	Today	Audit	Duration
0	Jacky	White	...	2019-09-13 12:00:00	2020-07-12 19:04:14. 449500	303 days 07:09:14. 449500	2019-12-13 12:00:00
1	Jane	Nize	...	2019-08-16 05:25:00	2020-07-12 19:04:14. 449500	331 days 13:44:14. 449500	2019-11-16 05:25:00
2	Henry	Tone	...	2019-05-06 12:00:00	2020-07-12 19:04:14. 449500	67days 07:09:14. 449500	2020-08-06 12:00:00
3	Desmond	Black	...	2019-05-01 05:25:00	2020-07-12 19:04:14. 449500	72 days 18:09:14. 449500	2020-08-01 01:00:00
4	Eileen	Musk	...	NaT	2020-07-12 19:04:14. 449500	NaT	NaT

4.8 Duplicate Values

Duplicate values are encountered very often in data cleaning and data analysis. To deal with them, they must be processed correctly, otherwise the results derived from the datasets may be unreliable. Pandas provides the *duplicated()* function to find all duplicate rows in a DataFrame based on a list of given columns names, and the *drop_duplicates()* function to drop duplicated rows.

```
duplicated(subset, keep)
drop_duplicates(subset, keep, inplace, ignore_index)

Arguments:
    subset: The list of columns for duplication check. (default is all columns)
    keep: {'first', 'last', False},(default is 'first')
            Determines which duplicates (if any) to mark at duplicated()
            Determines which duplicates (if any) to keep at drop_duplicates().
```

Now, let's see examples of how to find duplicate rows in DataFrames.

Finding duplicate rows by default

By default, the *duplicated()* function returns duplicate rows based on all columns in a DataFrame. The result below shows that df_credit has no duplicate rows.

```
df_credit.duplicated()
```

out:

0	False
1	False
2	False
3	False
4	False

dtype: bool

Finding duplicate rows based on selected columns

The example below shows that df_credit has duplicate credit card names. Since the *keep* option is set to "last", the result marks all rows with duplicate records as True, except for the last occurrence.

```
df_credit.duplicated('Card Name', keep = 'last')
```

out:

0	False
1	True
2	False
3	False
4	False

dtype: bool

Drop duplicate rows based on selected columns

This example shows how to drop all duplicate rows with the same credit card names aside from the first occurrence by setting *keep* to 'first'.

```
df_credit.drop_duplicates('Card Name', keep = 'first')
```

out:

	Card Name	Credit Score	First Name	Last Name	Credit Approval	Income	Approval Date	Segment
0	Infinite	825	Jacky	White	True	155000.62	2019-09-13 12:00:00	Excellent
1	Golden	812	Jane	Nize	True	120800.88	2019-08-16 05:25:00	Excellent
3	Silver	750	Desmond	Black	True	54000.00	2020-05-01 01:00:00	NaN
4	Dividend	620	Eileen	Musk	False	35000.00	NaT	Poor

4.9 Pivoting DataFrames

Pivoting or reshaping a DataFrame offers an alternative structure for the DataFrame, which contains identifier variables and its consecutive measurements. Pivoting is done by modifying the row-column structure of a DataFrame, which allows you to represent the relationship of rows and columns of a dataset in a different perspective. Pivoting is also sometimes referred to as "transposing". In certain cases, pivoting a DataFrame is done to make it easier to understand and analyze the relationship of the dataset. Pandas provides several pivoting methods which each have their own uses cases for analytical tasks, including *pivot()*, *melt()*, *stack()* and *unstack()*. In addition, Pandas also provides a pivoting tool, *pivot_table()*, which contains many versatile and powerful statistical summarization functions.

In pivoting terminology, datasets with more columns than rows are usually called wide data, and datasets with more rows than columns are usually called long data. Below, is a visual illustration of pivoting, using the DataFrame df_trans.

DataFrame Pivoting

Long Data

Card Number	Amount	Date
CN012	356.2	1/9/19
CN012	785	2/9/19
CN012	36.9	3/9/19
CN012	36.9	4/9/19
CN014	1.5	1/9/19
CN014	23.6	3/9/19
CN014	23.6	4/9/19
CN015	53.23	1/9/19
CN015	23.12	2/9/19
CN015	153.12	4/9/19

Wide Data

Card Number	1/9/19	2/9/19	3/9/19	4/9/19
CN012	356.2	785	36.9	36.9
CN014	1.5		23.6	23.6
CN015	53.23	23.12		153.1

Pivoting long data to wide data with a single index using pivot()

A use case of the *pivot()* function would be to pivot a long DataFrame over a single index converted from a column, into a wide DataFrame. The *pivot()* function would work to reshape the consecutive measurements of a column into row values, and transpose another column's values into column names, and finally the index as the row axis in the wide DataFrame.

The transactions DataFrame, df_trans, is a typical long DataFrame. It contains data of credit cards' transaction histories at different times, and has 4 columns - "Card Number", "Date", "Transactions" and "Amount". Each row represents the transaction summary of a credit card on a certain date. However the problem with the data being presented as long data, is that if you'd like to analyze transaction patterns in relation to Card Number-Date pairs for each card, it would make more sense to have a wide DataFrame, where each row is a consecutive transaction summary of a credit card at different times (don't worry if you don't understand, there will be a visualization below). The *pivot()* function generates this wide DataFrame by converting "Card Number" to a single row index label, transposing each "Date" value to a column name. This results in every cell value being transaction or amount associated with a Card Number-Date pair.

```
df_trans.pivot( index='Card Number', columns='Date', values = ['Transactions', 'Amount'])
```

original:

	Card Number	Date	Transactions	Amount
0	CN012	01/09/19	2	356.20
1	CN014	01/09/19	3	120.50
2	CN015	01/09/19	1	53.23
3	CN016	01/09/19	3	25.60
4	CN012	02/09/19	5	785.00
5	CN015	02/09/19	2	23.12
6	CN016	02/09/19	3	28.30
7	CN012	03/09/19	4	36.90
8	CN014	03/09/19	2	23.60
9	CN016	03/09/19	4	43.50

target:

Date	Transactions			Amount		
Card Number	01/09/19	02/09/19	03/09/19	01/09/19	02/09/19	03/09/19
CN012	2.0	5.0	4.0	356.20	785.00	36,9
CN014	3.0	NaN	2.0	120.50	NaN	23.6
CN015	1.0	2.0	NaN	53.23	23.12	NaN
CN016	3.0	3.0	4.0	25.60	28.30	43,5

Wide data to long data Using melt()

To unpivot a wide DataFrame into a long DataFrame, you may use the *melt()* function. The *melt()* function is used to unpivot the consecutive measurements (value_vars) in a row back to its original column values and column variable, along with the identifier variables (id_vars) as the row axis.

```
melt(DataFrame, id_vars, value_vars, var_name, value_name, col_level)

Arguments:
    id_vars: column used as identifier variables
    value_vars: column(s) to unpivot.
    var_names: name to use for the 'variable' column.
    value_names: name to use for the 'value' column
```

The example below shows how to use *melt()* to unpivot the first 4 records of df_trans. In this example, "Amount" and "Transactions" are unpivoted from the rows into the columns "Value" and "Variable" respectively.

```
df_trans[:4].melt(id_vars = ['Card Number', 'Date'] , value_vars= ['Amount', 'Transactions'] )
```

Original:

	Card Number	Transactions	Amount	Date
0	CN012	2	356.20	01/09/19
1	CN014	3	120.50	01/09/19
2	CN015	1	53.23	01/09/19
3	CN016	3	25.60	01/09/19

Target:

	Card Number	Date	Variable	Value
0	CN012	01/09/19	Amount	356.20
1	CN014	01/09/19	Amount	120.50
2	CN015	01/09/19	Amount	53.23
3	CN016	01/09/19	Amount	25.60
4	CN012	01/09/19	Transactions	2.00
5	CN014	01/09/19	Transactions	3.00
6	CN015	01/09/19	Transactions	1.00
7	CN016	01/09/19	Transactions	3.00

Pivoting multi-level index data using stack() and unstack()

It is quite common to use the *stack()* and *unstack()* functions for reshaping a multi-level index DataFrame. The *stack()* function reshapes a DataFrame by transposing the multi-level innermost column index into a new DataFrame with row labels in the inner-most level, whereas the *unstack()* function does the complete opposite. For example, assuming you have a 2-level hierarchical index on either axes of a DataFrame, stacking and unstacking this DataFrame would mean transposing the innermost column/**row** index to become the innermost **row**/column index, and the column/**row** values transposed to **row**/column values as well.

As a side note, if you think about it, *pivot()* does the exact same thing as *unstack()*, however it only unstacks a single index DataFrame. *pivot()* is almost like a special case of unstacking a DataFrame.

```
stack(self, level=, dropna=True)
unstack(self, level=, fill_value=None)

Arguments :
    level: Level(s) to stack from the column axis onto the index axis
    dropna: Whether to drop rows in the resulting with missing values
```

To illustrate how *stack()* and *unstack()* work, we'll create a multi-level row index DataFrame from df_trans and use the functions on it.

```python
df_multiindex = df_trans.sort_values(['Card Number','Date']).set_index(['Card Number','Date'])

# Multi-index long to wide using unstack
df_unstack = df_multiindex.unstack()

# Multi-index wide to long using unstack
df_unstack.stack()
```

Card Number	Date	Transactions	Amount
CN012	01/09/19	2.0	356.20
	02/09/19	5.0	785.00
	03/09/19	4.0	36.90
CN014	01/09/19	3.0	120.50
	03/09/19	2.0	23.60
CN015	01/09/19	1.0	53.23
	02/09/19	2.0	23.12
CN016	01/09/19	3.0	25.60
	02/09/19	3.0	28.30
	03/09/19	4.0	43.50

	Transactions			Amount		
Date	01/09/19	02/09/19	03/09/19	01/09/19	02/09/19	03/09/19
Card Number						
CN012	2.0	5.0	4.0	356.20	785.00	36.9
CN014	3.0	NaN	2.0	120.50	NaN	23.6
CN015	1.0	2.0	NaN	53.23	23.12	NaN
CN016	3.0	3.0	4.0	25.60	28.30	43.5

pivot_table()

pivot_table() is a powerful method which can be used to create a pivoted DataFrame with aggregated values from pivoted rows, such as the mean, median or other statistics. Its use is depicted below.

```
pivot_table(self, values, index, columns, aggfunc, fill_value, margins, dropna,
margins_name, observed)
Arguments :
    data: a DataFrame object.
    values: a column or a list of columns to aggregate.
    index: keys to group by on the pivot table index.
    columns: Keys to group by on the pivot table column.
    aggfunc: function to use for aggregation, defaulting to numpy.mean.
```

The example below to obtains the mean and sum of the pivoted data

```
df_trans.pivot_table( values='Amount', index=['Card Number' ],
          columns=['Date'] ,aggfunc=[ np.mean ,np.sum] )
```

out:

	mean			sum		
Date	**2019-09-01**	**2019-09-02**	**2019-09-03**	**2019-09-01**	**2019-09-02**	**2019-09-03**
Card Number						
CN012	356.20	785.00	36.9	356.20	785.00	36.9
CN014	120.50	NaN	23.6	120.50	NaN	23.6
CN015	53.23	23.12	NaN	53.23	23.12	NaN
CN016	25.60	28.30	43.5	25.60	28.30	43.5

4.10 Grouping DataFrames

Grouping and aggregation are basic building blocks of data science for efficiently extracting insights from large datasets. Frequently, data scientists will apply a technique know as **split-apply-combine**. To do this, first, you divide a large dataset into smaller groups based on specific conditions, then you apply changes or aggregations, like sum(), mean(), and median(), to each group, then finally combine the results back into a new data structure with assigned labels. The aggregation functions used reduce the dimensions of the returned results for exploring the nature of the data. Pandas implements grouping using the *groupby()* function.

```
groupby(by, axis, level, as_index, sort, group_keys)

Arguments :
    by: the list of labels used to determine the groups for the groupby
    level: If the axis is a multi-index, group by a particular level or levels.
```

A pythonic way to apply the *groupby()* function is to break the **split-apply-combine** process into 3 parts: conditions of groups (Group), the feature(s) to be aggregated (Feature), and functions or aggregations that will be executed (aggregation).

```
groupby(['Group'])['Feature'].aggregation()
```

Applying functions with groupby()

The example below calculates the total summation of transactions for each card. Thus, to do this, "Card Number" will be used as the condition of the group, "Amount" and "Transactions" as features for aggregation, and sum() as the aggregation function.

```
df_trans.groupby('Card Number')['Amount','Transactions'].sum()
```

out:

Card Number	Amount	Transaction
CN012	1215.00	17
CN014	167.70	7
CN015	229.47	4
CN016	97.40	10

Multiple aggregation functions

You can apply multiple aggregation functions to the selected features by passing a list of aggregation functions to the *agg()* function.

```
df_trans.groupby('Card Number')['Amount'].agg([np.sum, np.mean, np.std])
```

out:

Card Number	sum	mean	std
CN012	1215.00	303.750000	354.386987
CN014	167.70	55.900000	55.945241
CN015	229.47	76.490000	68.049766
CN016	97.40	32.466667	9.650043

Different aggregations to different columns

By passing a dictionary with a {'feature': function} structure to the *agg()* function, *groupby()* will apply your aggregation functions to the values of the specified features.

```
df_trans.groupby('Card Number').agg({'Transactions':['min', 'max'], 'Amount':
'mean'})
```

out:

	Transactions		Amount
	min	max	mean
Card Number			
CN012	2	6	303.750000
CN014	2	3	55.900000
CN015	1	2	76.490000
CN016	3	4	32.466667

Applying user-defined function

Using *apply()* alongside the *groupby()* function, you will be able to apply your own aggregation functions.

```
def mean_plus_std(x):
    return x.mean() + 1.96 * x.std()

df_trans.groupby('Card Number')['Transactions','Amount'].apply(
mean_plus_std)
```

out:

	Transactions	Amount
Card Number		
CN012	7.597337	998.348495
CN014	3.464940	165.552673
CN015	2.464940	209.867542
CN016	4.464940	51.380751

Below are some common aggregation functions can be applied to the *groupby()* function directly:

Function	Description
mean()	Compute mean of groups
sum()	Compute sum of group values
size()	Compute group sizes
count()	Compute count of group
std()	Standard deviation of groups

var()	Compute variance of groups
sem()	Standard error of the mean of groups
describe()	Generates descriptive statistics
first()	Compute first of group values
last()	Compute last of group values
nth()	Take nth value, or a subset if n is a list
min()	Compute min of group values
max()	Compute max of group values

4.11 Shifting and Rolling

Shifting and rolling are popular techniques used by data scientists to analyze time series data, regarding the difference of data between different periods, or to smooth out data using the moving average between periods. To accomplish this, Pandas provides the *shift()* function to shift the index by a desired number of periods with an optional time frequency, and the *rolling()* function for calculating the statistics on a rolling window. Both functions are very helpful and make a data scientist's task much easier with the fantastic Python data-centric ecosystem.

shift()

The shift() function shifts specified values up or down (right or left) and keeps other values unchanged along a specified axis in a DataFrame. This function is similar to the LAG() and LEAD() functions in SQL. The scalar number of shifts to be made over the desired axis is called periods, which is a parameter of the shift function. As well, *shift()* can either shift a whole DataFrame or just specified columns up or down (right or left). Additionally, it can shift columns within groups up or down.

```
shift(periods, freq, axis, fill_value)

Arguments:
    periods : Number of periods to shift, can be positive or negative
    axis : {0 or 'index', 1 or 'columns'}
    fill_value: The scalar value to use for newly introduced missing values.
```

Shifting a whole DataFrame by 1 period

By default, DataFrames shift downwards along the specified index.

```
df_credit.shift(1)
```

original:

	First Name	Last Name	Credit Score	Credit Approval	Card Name	Income	Approval Date
0	Jacky	White	825	True	Infinite	155000.62	2019-09-13
1	Jane	Nize	812	True	Golden	120800.88	2019-08-16
2	Henry	Tone	780	True	Golden	98000.58	2020-05-06
3	Desmond	Black	750	True	Silver	54000.00	2020-05-01
4	Eileen	Musk	620	False	Dividend	35000.00	NaT

out:

	First Name	Last Name	Credit Score	Credit Approval	Card Name	Income	Approval Date
0	NaN	NaN	NaN	NaN	NaN	NaN	NaT
1	Jane	Nize	812	True	Golden	120800.88	2019-08-16
2	Henry	Tone	780	True	Golden	98000.58	2020-05-06
3	Desmond	Black	750	True	Silver	54000.00	2020-05-01
4	Eileen	Musk	620	False	Dividend	35000.00	NaT

Shifting the column by 1 period

If the *shift()* function is used to shift a single column left or right, a new Series object is created. If shifted several columns, a new sub DataFrame is created.

```
df_credit['New Score'] = df_credit['Credit Score'].shift(1)
```

out:

	First Name	Last Name	Credit Score	Credit Approval	Card Name	Income	Approval Date	New Score
0	Jacky	White	825	True	Infinite	155000.62	2019-09-13	NaN
1	Jane	Nize	812	True	Golden	120800.88	2019-08-16	825.0
2	Henry	Tone	780	True	Golden	98000.58	2020-05-06	810.0
3	Desmond	Black	750	True	Silver	54000.00	2020-05-01	780.0
4	Eileen	Musk	620	False	Dividend	35000.00	NaT	750.0

Shifting a column by 1 period within a group

When working with the *groupby()* function, *shift()* works as an aggregation function, and shifts specified columns within a group. The example below shows that a new column "New_trans" is created by shifting the column "Transactions" down by 1 period, within the "CardNumber" group.

```
df_trans.sort_values('Card Number', inplace=True)
df_trans['New_trans']=df_trans.groupby(['Card Number'])['Transactions'].shift()
```

out:

Card Number	Date	Transactions	Amount
CN012	2019-09-01	2	356.2
CN012	2019-09-02	5	785
CN012	2019-09-03	4	36.9
CN014	2019-09-01	3	120.5
CN014	2019-09-03	2	23.6
CN015	2019-09-01	1	53.23
CN015	2019-09-02	2	23.12
CN016	2019-09-01	3	25.6
CN016	2019-09-02	3	28.3
CN016	2019-09-03	4	43.5

Card Number	Date	Transactions	Amount	New_trans
CN012	2019-09-01	2	356.2	NaN
CN012	2019-09-02	5	785	2.0
CN012	2019-09-03	4	36.9	5.0
CN014	2019-09-01	3	120.5	NaN
CN014	2019-09-03	2	23.6	3.0
CN015	2019-09-01	1	53.23	NaN
CN015	2019-09-02	2	23.12	1.0
CN016	2019-09-01	3	25.6	NaN
CN016	2019-09-02	3	28.3	3.0
CN016	2019-09-03	4	43.5	3.0

rolling()

As the name implies, the *rolling()* function provides rolling window calculations. It provides a convenient and compact way to shift data, then perform calculations on the shifted data.

```
rolling(self, window, min_periods, center, win_type, on, axis, closed)
```

Arguments:
   window: Size of the moving window
   win_typestr: Provide a window type. Default is evenly weighted.

Rolling summation for rolling window = 2

Here, we use df_credit as an example to show how to calculate the rolling-sum of "Credit Score" within 2 moving windows.

```
df_credit['Scores'] = df_credit['Credit Score'].rolling(2).sum()
```

out:

	First Name	Last Name	Credit Score	Credit Approval	Card Name	Income	Approval Date	Scores
0	Jacky	White	825	True	Infinite	155000.62	2019-09-13	NaN
1	Jane	Nize	810	True	Golden	120800.88	2019-08-16	1635.0
2	Henry	Tone	780	True	Golden	98000.58	2020-05-06	1590
3	Desmond	Black	750	True	Silver	54000.00	2020-05-01	1530.0
4	Eileen	Musk	620	False	Dividend	35000.00	NaT	1370

4.12 The apply() Function

Often, you may encounter scenarios in which complex business logic, which includes many intermediate steps, needs to be applied on a DataFrame, such as deriving a new column from other columns based on certain conditions. To make this easier, Pandas provides the *apply()* function which serves as convenient and easy way to handle this job, to avoid much of the tedious intermediate work. The *apply()* function can call a user-defined function or a lambda function, and passes the Series from the row or column contents to the function according to the axis argument, and returns a modified copy of the DataFrame with new contents returned by the called function.

apply(func, axis, broadcast, raw, reduce, result_typee, args, **kwds)

Arguments:
    func : Function to be applied to each column or row.
    axis : the axis to be applied, {0: column, 1: row}
    args : tuple / list of arguments to passed to function.

The general use of *apply()* function is as follows:

    Step 1: Define a function that will apply your business logic on the row or column values that you're working with.

    Step 2: Use the apply function along with a user-defined or lambda function on the row or column by setting axis = 1 or 0. The default axis is the column.

Applying a user-defined function

To apply a user-defined function on a DataFrame, you will need to pass the function and axis arguments to DataFrame.apply(), which will then return a modified copy of the DataFrame constructed with new contents returned by

the called function. The following example adds 3 to each item in the
DataFrame, df_raw.

```
def add_3(x):
    return x + 3
df_raw = pd.DataFrame({'A': [1,3], 'B':[2,4]})
df_raw.apply(add_3)
```

out:

	df_raw		after apply function	
	A	**B**	**A**	**B**
0	1	2	0 4	5
1	3	4	1 6	7

Applying a user-defined function on a specific column

To apply a user defined function to a specific column, you only need specify
the column name for the DataFrame. The example below creates a new
column "C" by adding 3 to the specified column "B" in df_raw.

```
df_raw['C'] = df_raw['B'].apply(add_3 )
```

out:

	A	**B**	**C**
0	1	2	5
1	3	4	7

Applying lambda functions

Lambda functions are widely used in Python and other programming
languages, acting as anonymous functions which do not require a name, and
performs small tasks with little code. It is a small function which contains a
single expression and adds functional features to Python.

In Python, a Lambda function consists of the following three parts:

- Keyword *lambda*

- Bound variable/argument
- Body or expression

The keyword is mandatory, and it must be **lambda**, whereas the arguments and the body expressions are based on the function's requirements.

Applying lambda functions on a DataFrame

Just like applying a user-defined function on a DataFrame, to apply a lambda function, you'll need to pass the lambda function directly to the *apply()* function along with other arguments. The example below shows how to add 5 to each item of the DataFrame df_raw.

```
df_raw.apply(lambda x : x + 5)
```

out:

	A	B
0	6	7
1	8	9

Applying a function on a specific column

If you specify a column of a DataFrame when invoking the *apply()* function, the lambda or user-defined function will only be applied to the specified column. The following example creates a new column "C" by adding 5 to every value in the column "B".

```
df_raw['C'] = df_raw['B'].apply(lambda x : x + 5)
```

out:

	A	B	C
0	1	2	7
1	3	4	9

Chapter 5   Merging and Concatenating Multiple DataFrames

In previous chapters, you've learned how to manipulate a single DataFrame on its own. In this chapter, you'll be introduced to data manipulation operations across multiple DataFrames: merging and concatenation. Each operation combines two or more DataFrames along a specified axis, either rows or columns. Axes are also usually referred to as dimensions - the horizontal dimension representing rows, and vertical dimension representing columns. Horizontal operations combine DataFrames through common columns' values, row indices, or subsets of DataFrames which are derived from conditions based on values of another DataFrame. Vertical operations combine DataFrames by aligning common columns at the mean time.

Merging two datasets is an instance of a horizontal operation, which joins two datasets together by aligning rows based on common row attributes, or the index. Concatenation in Python can include both horizontal and vertical operations on DataFrames.

5.1 Introducing merge() Function

The words merge and join are often used interchangeably in many programming languages, as both functions work by combining datasets horizontally. Thus, most of time, a merge is also referred to as a join. As well, people usually call the left side data "left table" (left) and the right side data "right table" (right). In Pandas, there are four types of DataFrame merge/joins: inner join, left outer join, right outer join and full outer join. These four joins are standard across most databases and data analytical languages (Python,

SQL, SAS and R). The table below illustrates the match relationship between merging methods in Pandas and SQL join:

Merge method	SQL Join Name	Description
inner	INNER JOIN	use intersection of keys from both frames
left	LEFT OUTER JOIN	use keys from left frame only
right	RIGHT OUTER JOIN	use keys from right frame only
outer	FULL OUTER JOIN	use union of keys from both frames

- **Inner join** – The default join in Pandas, only keeps rows where the key value exists in both left and right DataFrames.
- **Left outer join** – Keep all rows in the left DataFrame and the data from the right DataFrame with matched keys. Fills in empty values elsewhere.
- **Right outer join** – Keep all rows in the right DataFrame and matched data from the left DataFrame. Fills in empty values elsewhere.
- **Full outer join** – A full outer join returns all the rows from the left DataFrame and the right DataFrame, and matches up rows where possible, with filled in empty values elsewhere.

Don't worry if you're finding it hard to grasp the different joins. To help you understand them, below is a visual diagram that illustrates how the four merges/joins work. The figures follow this convention:

- The blue color indicates rows that are present in the merge result
- The yellow color indicates rows that are excluded from the result
- The green color indicates not matched values that are replaced with NaNs in the result

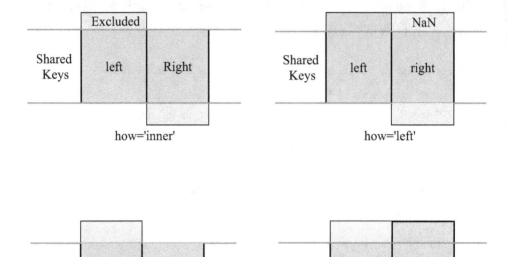

Pandas provides several functions, such as *merge()*, *join()*, and *concat()*, to merge DataFrames for better adaptation to the merging relationship among DataFrames. While both *merge()* and *join()* can do all kinds of joins, *concat()* can only work on inner and full outer joins. The dilemma between choosing how and when to combine DataFrames using them is as below:

- join: merging DataFrames on index or key columns
- merge: merging DataFrames on common columns or indices
- concat: merging across rows

5.2 Merging DataFrames Using merge()

Pandas provides both the *merge()* and *join()* functions, which perform similar tasks – that is, merging DataFrames. By default, the *join()* function combines DataFrames using the indices of each DataFrame to perform a left join, while the *merge()* function matches the common key columns to perform an inner join. Furthermore, the *merge()* function provides more versatile methods to merge DataFrames.

merge(right, how, on, left_on, right_on, left_index, right_index, sort, suffixes, copy, indicator, validate)

Arguments:
  right: A DataFrame or series to be merged with the calling DataFrame
  how: Merge type, values are: left, right, outer, inner. Default is 'inner'.
  On: Column name on which merge will be done.
  left_on: Specific column names in left DataFrame
  right_on: Specific column names in right DataFrame
  left_index: If True will choose index from left DataFrame as join key.
  right_index: If True will choose index from right DataFrame as join key.
  suffixes: Suffex to be applied on overlapping columns in DataFrames.

Frequently used merge methods:

1. Merging on common columns with different join types

left.merge(right, on=['key_1',..., 'key_n'], how='left')
left.merge(right, on=['key_1',..., 'key_n'], how='right')
left.merge(right, on=['key_1',..., 'key_n'], how='outer')
left.merge(right, on=['key_1',..., 'key_n'], how='left')

2. Merging on different column names using "left_on" and "right_on" option

left.merge(right, left_on=['l_key_1',..., 'l_key_n'], right_on=['r_key_1',..., 'r_key_n'])

3. Merging on index using "left_index" and "right_index" option

```
left.merge(right, left_index=True, right_index=True)
```

4. Merging on index of one DataFrame, column(s) of another.

```
left.merge(right, left_on='key1', right_index=True)
```

merge() on common columns

As a quick start, *merge()* takes the left and right DataFrames' matching rows based on the list of columns passed to the 'on' option, and performs different types of merges (left, right, outer and inner) based on the value passed to the "How" option. Below is a visual illustration of *merge()* using df_cards and df_trans as example.

"left" DataFrame   "right" DataFrame

```
result=pd.merge( df_cards,
                 df_trans,
                 left_on='Card Number',
                 right_on='Card Number',
                 how='left'}
```

"right_on" specifies   "how" can be one   "left_on" specifies
matching column   of: {left, right, inner, matching column
name(s) in right   outer}   name(s) in left
DataFrame   DataFrame

Below are some examples to show how *merge()* works using the subset of the DataFrames df_cards and df_trans, where df_cards serves as the left table and df_trans serves as the right table. To help you better understand, here is the sample data used in following.

```
df_cards_1 = df_cards[:3]
df_trans_1 = df_trans[df_trans['Card Number'].isin (['CN014', 'CN015',
'CN016'])]
```

	First Name	Last Name	Card Number	Limitation	Effective Date
0	Jacky	White	CN012	10000	2019-09-13 12:00:00
1	Jane	Nize	CN014	9800	2019-08-16 05:25:00
2	Henry	Tone	CN015	12000	2019-09-13 12:00:00

right table: df_trans_1:

	Card Number	Date	Transactions	Amount
1	CN014	2019-09-01	3	120.50
2	CN015	2019-09-01	1	53.23
3	CN016	2019-09-01	3	25.60
5	CN015	2019-09-02	2	23.12
6	CN016	2019-09-02	3	28.30
8	CN014	2019-09-03	2	23.60
9	CN016	2019-09-03	4	43.50

Merging on common columns by default (inner join)

The example below shows how to perform the default merge, which is an inner join. The result of the merge is a new DataFrame with rows from both input DataFrames where 'Card Number' is the same.

```
df_cards_1.merge(df_trans_1 , on = 'Card Number')
```

out:

	First Name	Last Name	Card Number	Limitation	Effective Date	Transactions	Amount	Date
0	Jane	Nize	CN014	9800	2019-08-16 05:25:00	3	120.50	2019-09-01
1	Jane	Nize	CN014	9800	2019-08-16 05:25:00	2	23.60	2019-09-03
2	Henry	Tone	CN015	12000	2019-09-13 12:00:00	1	53.23	2019-09-01
3	Henry	Tone	CN015	12000	2019-09-13 12:00:00	2	23.12	2019-09-02

Merging on common columns by default (inner join)

This example shows how to merge on common columns of the left and right DataFrames using the left join method. This is done by specifying "how = ' left ' ". The result is a new DataFrame which includes all rows from the left DataFrame, and matched data from the right DataFrame. All non-matched rows from the right DataFrame are filled as "NaN".

```
df_cards_1.merge(df_trans_1 , on = 'Card Number', how='left')
```

out:

	First Name	Last Name	Card Number	Limitation	Effective Date	Date	Transactions	Amount
0	Jacky	White	CN012	10000	2019-09-13 12:00:00	NaT	NaN	NaN
1	Jane	Nize	CN014	9800	2019-08-16 05:25:00	2019-09-01	3	120.50
2	Jane	Nize	CN014	9800	2019-08-16 05:25:00	2019-09-03	2	23.60
3	Henry	Tone	CN015	12000	2019-09-13 12:00:00	2019-09-01	1	53.23
4	Henry	Tone	CN015	12000	2019-09-13 12:00:00	2019-09-02	2	23.12

Merging on indices

This example shows how to merge on the indices of DataFrames, which is done by setting both "left_index" and "right_index" as True. Since the right DataFrame has only 3 records, therefore the result will only have 3 records (index of 0, 1 and 2 in both DataFrames).

```
df_cards_1.merge(df_trans_1 , left_index = True, right_index = True,
how='left')
```

out:

	First Name	Last Name	Card Number_x	Limitation	Effective Date	Card Number_y	Date	Trans actions	Amount
0	Jacky	White	CN012	10000	2019-09-13 12:00:00	NaN	NaT	NaN	NaN
1	Jane	Nize	CN014	9800	2019-08-16 05:25:00	CN014	2019-09-01	3	120.50
2	Henry	Tone	CN015	12000	2019-09-13 12:00:00	CN015	2019-09-01	1	53.23

Multiway merging on columns and indices

This example shows a hybrid merge by using the index of the left DataFrame and column of the right DataFrame. To do this, you'll need to specify the index and column for both DataFrames respectively. Before we perform our merge, we'll need to set the index of our left DataFrame to 'Card Number' first.

```
df_cards_1 = df_cards_1.set_index('Card Number')
df_cards_1.merge(df_trans_1 , left_index = True, right_on = 'Card Number',
how='inner')
```

out:

	First Name	Last Name	Limitation	Effective Date	Card Number	Date	Transactions	Amount
1	Jane	Nize	9800	2019-09-13 12:00:00	CN014	2019-09-01	3	120.50
8	Jane	Nize	9800	2019-08-16 05:25:00	CN014	2019-09-03	2	23.60
2	Henry	Tone	12000	2019-08-16 05:25:00	CN015	2019-09-01	1	53.23
5	Henry	Tone	12000	2019-06-01 12:00:00	CN015	2019-09-02	2	23.12

5.3 Merging DataFrames Using join()

By default, the *join()* function conducts a left join on the indices of the left and right DataFrames. It can also merge DataFrames by common columns, like *merge()* does, through setting the "on" option using the common columns as the key join values. In fact, *join()* function provides a more efficient way to merge DataFrames than the *merge()* function does, at the cost of some versatility.

```
join(other, on=, how=, lsuffix=, rsuffix=, sort)
Arguments :
  other: the right DataFrame or Series
  on: the common key value in the both DataFrames for join
  how: {'left', 'right', 'outer', 'inner'}, method for merge
  lsuffix/rsuffix: suffix to use from left/right frame's overlapping columns
```

join() on index

The example below shows that the *join()* function merges the DataFrames df_cards and df_trans on their indices by default. The result includes all the data from de_cards and df_trans with matched indices (index 0-5). In addition, the lsuffix option allows you to rename the column "Card Number" of df_cards to "Card Number_l" to disguish it from the column "Card Number" of df_trans.

```
df_cards.join(df_trans, lsuffix = '_l')
```

out:

	First Name	Last Name	Card Number_I	Limitation	Effective Date	Card Number	Date	Trans actions	Amou nt
0	Jacky	White	CN012	10000	2019-09-13 12:00:00	CN012	2019-09-01	2	356.20
1	Jane	Nize	CN014	9800	2019-08-16 05:25:00	CN014	2019-09-01	3	120.50
2	Henry	Tone	CN015	12000	2019-09-13 12:00:00	CN015	2019-09-01	1	53.23
3	Desmond	Black	CN016	5000	2019-08-16 05:25:00	CN016	2019-09-01	3	25.60
4	Henry	Tone	CN015	15000	2019-05-01 12:00:00	CN012	2019-09-02	5	785.00
5	Desmond	Black	CN016	2000	2019-05-01 01:00:00	CN015	2019-09-02	2	23.12

join() on common key columns

By default, the *join()* function merges two DataFrames based on indices, however, it also able to merge DataFrames based on the common key column values like the *merge()* function. This can be done either by setting the common key columns as indices in both Dataframes, or by setting the common column as the index for one DataFrame and setting the parameter *on* as the common column of the other DataFrame.

The example below shows how to use the *join()* function to merge two DataFrames on common key columns by setting the common columns as indices for both DataFrames.

```
df_cards.set_index('Card Number').join(df_trans.set_index('Card Number'),
how = 'left' )
```

out:

Card Number	First Name	Last Name	Limitation	Effective Date	Date	Transactions	Amount
CN012	Jacky	White	10000	2019-09-13 12:00:00	2019-09-01	2	356.2
CN012	Jacky	White	10000	2019-09-13 12:00:00	2019-09-02	5	785
CN012	Jacky	White	10000	2019-09-13 12:00:00	2019-09-03	4	36.9
CN014	Jane	Nize	9800	2019-08-16 05:25:00	2019-09-01	3	120.5

CN014	Jane	Nize	9800	2019-08-16 05:25:00	2019-09-03	2	23.6
CN015	Henry	Tone	12000	2019-09-13 12:00:00	2019-09-01	1	53.23
CN015	Henry	Tone	12000	2019-09-13 12:00:00	2019-09-02	2	23.12
CN015	Henry	Tone	15000	2020-05-01 12:00:00	2019-09-01	1	53.23
CN015	Henry	Tone	15000	2020-05-01 12:00:00	2019-09-02	2	23.12
CN016	Desmond	Black	5000	2019-08-16 05:25:00	2019-09-01	3	25.6
CN016	Desmond	Black	5000	2019-08-16 05:25:00	2019-09-02	3	28.3
CN016	Desmond	Black	5000	2019-08-16 05:25:00	2019-09-03	4	43.5
CN016	Desmond	Black	2000	2020-05-01 12:00:00	2019-09-01	3	25.6
CN016	Desmond	Black	2000	2020-05-01 12:00:00	2019-09-02	3	28.3
CN016	Desmond	Black	2000	2020-05-01 12:00:00	2019-09-03	4	43.5

5.4 Merging DataFrames Using concat()

The concat() function works for both horizontal merging and vertical
concatenation of DataFrames. By default, the *concat()* function returns a new
DataFrame which is the result of concatenating the two DataFrames along the
vertical dimension, combining overlapping columns, and filling columns
outside of the intersection with NaN values. Additionally, the *concat()*
function can be used as an alternative merging method to the index-based
join() function, which merges DataFrames along the horizontal dimension by
passing 1 to the *axis* option. However, *conca*t() only offers full outer joins and
inner joins to combine DataFrames. The outer join option returns all
overlapping row indices or columns, and NaN for values outside of the
intersection. The inner join option only returns the combined DataFrames with
overlapping row indices or columns only.

concat(objs, , axis, join, ignore_index, keys, levels, names, verify_integrity, sort, copy)

Arguments :
   objs: a sequence or mapping of Series or DataFrame objects
   axis: The axis to concatenate along. (default 0) {0/'index', 1/'columns'}
   join: join method, (default 'outer'), {'inner', 'outer'}

A supplemental visual of pd.concat([left, right], axis =1) is shown below.

Merging DataFrames using concat()

The example below shows how to merge DataFrames using *concat()* with the inner join option. The output of the inner join is a combination of all columns from both DataFrames with shared row indices.

pd.concat([df_cards, df_trans], axis = 1, join ='inner')

out:

	First Name	Last Name	Card Number	...	Card Number	Date	Transactions	Amount
0	Jacky	White	CN012	...	CN012	2019-09-01	2	356.20
1	Jane	Nize	CN014	...	CN014	2019-09-01	3	120.50
2	Henry	Tone	CN015	...	CN015	2019-09-01	1	53.23
3	Desmond	Black	CN016	...	CN016	2019-09-01	3	25.60
4	Henry	Tone	CN015	...	CN015	2019-09-02	5	785.00
5	Desmond	Black	CN016	...	CN016	2019-09-02	2	23.12

Here's an example of merging DataFrames using *concat()* with the outer join option.

```
pd.concat([df_cards, df_trans], axis = 1, join ='outer')
```

out:

	First Name	Last Name	Card Number	Limitation	Effective Date	Card Number	Date	Transactions	Amount
0	Jacky	White	CN012	10000.0	2019-09-13 12:00:00	CN012	2019-09-01	2	356.20
1	Jane	Nize	CN014	9800.0	2019-08-16 05:25:00	CN014	2019-09-01	3	120.50
2	Henry	Tone	CN015	12000.0	2019-09-13 12:00:00	CN015	2019-09-01	1	53.23
3	Desmond	Black	CN016	5000.0	2019-08-16 05:25:00	CN016	2019-09-01	3	25.60
4	Henry	Tone	CN015	15000.0	2019-05-01 12:00:00	CN012	2019-09-02	5	785
5	Desmond	Black	CN016	2000.0	2019-05-01 01:00:00	CN015	2019-09-02	2	23.12
6	NaN	NaN	NaN	NaN	NaT	CN016	2019-09-02	3	28.30
7	NaN	NaN	NaN	NaN	NaT	CN012	2019-09-03	4	36.90
8	NaN	NaN	NaN	NaN	NaT	CN014	2019-09-03	2	23.60
9	NaN	NaN	NaN	NaN	NaT	CN016	2019-09-03	4	43.50

5.5 Concatenating DataFrames Using concat()

Concatenating can be defined as stacking or appending one DataFrame vertically under another. By default, the *concat()* function works by concatenating DataFrames along the vertical dimension. It offers the options of either a full outer join, which keeps overlapping columns and fills columns outside of the intersection with NaN values, or an inner join, which only keeps overlapping columns. By default, if you don't specify the 'join' option, *concat()* with perform an outer join.

Below is a supplemental visual of vertical concatenations of DataFrames using pd.concat([upper, lower], axis =0), for the join options of "outer" and "inner" respectively.

```
pd.concat([upper, lower], axis=0, sort=False, join='outer')
pd.concat([upper, lower], axis=0, sort=False, join='inner')
```

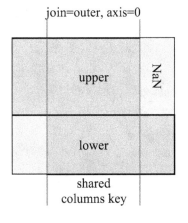

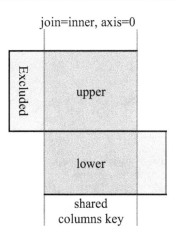

Concatenating DataFrames using concat() by default outer join

The example below concatenates DataFrames df_card and df_trans using the default outer join. The result keeps all rows from both DataFrames by appending the common columns "Card Number", while the other columns are filled with NaN.

```
pd.concat([df_cards, df_trans], axis = 0, sort=False )
```

out:

	First Name	Last Name	Card Number	...	Date	Transactions	Amount
0	Jacky	White	CN012	...	NaT	NaN	NaN
1	Jane	Nize	CN014	...	NaT	NaN	NaN
2	Henry	Tone	CN015	...	NaT	NaN	NaN
3	Desmond	Black	CN016	...	NaT	NaN	NaN
4	Henry	Tone	CN015	...	NaT	NaN	NaN
5	Desmond	Black	CN016	...	NaT	NaN	NaN
0	NaN	NaN	CN012	...	2019-09-01	2.0	356.20
1	NaN	NaN	CN014	...	2019-09-01	3.0	120.50
2	NaN	NaN	CN015	...	2019-09-01	1.0	53.23
3	NaN	NaN	CN016	...	2019-09-01	3.0	25.60
4	NaN	NaN	CN012	...	2019-09-02	5.0	785.00
5	NaN	NaN	CN015	...	2019-09-02	2.0	23.12
6	NaN	NaN	CN016	...	2019-09-02	3.0	28.30
7	NaN	NaN	CN012	...	2019-09-03	4.0	36.90
8	NaN	NaN	CN014	...	2019-09-03	2.0	23.60
9	NaN	NaN	CN016	...	2019-09-03	4.0	43.50

Concatenating DataFrames using concat() by inner join

The example below shows how to use the *concat()* function to concatenate df_card and df_trans with the inner join option, which only keeps common columns between both DataFrames.

```
pd.concat([df_cards_1 ,df_trans_1],axis = 0,join ='inner', sort=False )
```

out:

Card Number
CN012
CN014
CN015
CN014
CN015
CN016
CN015
CN016
CN014
CN016
CN014
CN015

5.6 Concatenating DataFrames Using append()

Pandas also provides the *append()* function, which works for stacking DataFrames just like the *concat()* function. It is simple to use when there are only two DataFrames that need to be concatenated by an outer join. The output is equivalent to the output from *concat()* function.

```
append(self, other, ignore_index, verify_integrity, sort)
```

Concatenating DataFrames using append()

```
df_cards.append(df_trans,sort=False)
# It is equivalent to
pd.concat([df_cards ,df_trans],sort=False)
```

out:

	First Name	Last Name	Card Number	...	Date	Transactions	Amount
0	Jacky	White	CN012	...	NaT	NaN	NaN
1	Jane	Nize	CN014	...	NaT	NaN	NaN
2	Henry	Tone	CN015	...	NaT	NaN	NaN
3	Desmond	Black	CN016	...	NaT	NaN	NaN
4	Henry	Tone	CN015	...	NaT	NaN	NaN
5	Desmond	Black	CN016	...	NaT	NaN	NaN
0	NaN	NaN	CN012	...	2019-09-01	2.0	356.20
1	NaN	NaN	CN014	...	2019-09-01	3.0	120.50
2	NaN	NaN	CN015	...	2019-09-01	1.0	53.23
3	NaN	NaN	CN016	...	2019-09-01	3.0	25.60
4	NaN	NaN	CN012	...	2019-09-02	5.0	785.00
5	NaN	NaN	CN015	...	2019-09-02	2.0	23.12
6	NaN	NaN	CN016	...	2019-09-02	3.0	28.30
7	NaN	NaN	CN012	...	2019-09-03	4.0	36.90
8	NaN	NaN	CN014	...	2019-09-03	2.0	23.60
9	NaN	NaN	CN016	...	2019-09-03	4.0	43.50

Chapter 6   Querying DataFrames Using Pandasql

For those of you who are new to Pandas but come from a SQL background, the package pandasql offers you a more familiar way of manipulating DataFrames through applying SQL queries directly onto the DataFrame, which allows you to perform complex tasks. The slogan of Pandasql is "Make python speak SQL", as it allows you to query DataFrames using SQL syntax and think with a SQL-oriented mindset. It is very similar to *sqldf()* in R. Pandasql is powered by SQLite3, therefore, you can do almost anything that is possible in the standard SQL language, and provides a convenient way to take advantage of the strengths of both languages. This chapter briefly introduces using pandasql to query DataFrames and syntax comparison between Pandas and pandasql.

6.1 Pandasql

The pandasql package can be installed directly through pip.

Installation

```
pip install -U pandasql
```

The main function used in pandasql is *sqldf()*. It accepts 2 parameters: a SQL query string, and a set of session/environment variables (locals() or globals()), where locals() and globals() are built-in python functions that are used to return the corresponding namespace.

To avoid the hassle of passing *locals()* or *globals()* all the time, data scientists usually define a short helper function to do this, as shown below (*pysqldf()*).

```
from pandasql import sqldf
pysqldf = lambda q: sqldf(q, globals())
```

The examples below illustrate how pandasql and helper function work. The syntax and outputs are straightforward if you have experience with SQL.

Subquery of columns

```
q = '''SELECT [First Name],
            [Last Name],
            [Credit Score],
              [Credit Approval]
       FROM df_credit
       WHERE [Credit Approval] = 1 ;
    '''
pysqldf(q)
```

out:

	First Name	Last Name	Credit Score	Credit Approval
0	Jacky	White	825	1
1	Jane	Nize	810	1
2	Henry	Tone	780	1
3	Desmond	Black	750	1

Left join of DataFrames

```
q = '''SELECT a.*,
          b.[Card Number]
       FROM df_credit a
       left join
          df_cards b
       on a.[First Name] = b.[First Name] and
          a.[Last Name] = b.[Last Name];
    '''
pysqldf(q).head(4)
```

out:

	First Name	Last Name	Credit Score	Credit Approval	Card Name	Income	Approval Date	Card Number
0	Jacky	White	825	1	Infinite	155000.62	2019-09-13	CN012
1	Jane	Nize	810	1	Golden	120800.88	2019-08-16	CN014
2	Henry	Tone	780	1	Golden	98000.58	2020-05-06	CN015
3	Henry	Tone	780	1	Golden	98000.58	2020-05-06	CN015

Pandasql working with parameters

Usually when you need to dynamically query a DataFrame, you can use placeholder values to pass the associated values to the query, via a tuple with the "%" operator. In this case, %s acts a placeholder for a string and %d acts as a placeholder for a number or decimal. The example below uses the tuple %(credit_score) to pass the value of credit_score. You may set the value of credit_score to any value you'd like, and the query will dynamically generate an output according to the input value. In this example, the value of credit_score is set to 750, thus the output returns the requested column with "Credit Score" > 750.

```
credit_score = 750
q = "'SELECT [First Name],
        [Last Name],
        [Credit Score],
        [Credit Approval]
    FROM df_credit
    where [Credit Score] > %d ;
    "'%(credit_score)
pysqldf(q)
```

out:

	First Name	Last Name	Credit Score	Credit Approval
0	Jacky	White	825	1
1	Jane	Nize	810	1
2	Henry	Tone	780	1

107

6.2 Comparison between Pandas and SQL

Both Pandas and SQL can work on querying and manipulating table data. Below is a summary of comparisons between Pandas and SQL.

SELECT, WHERE, DISTINCT, LIMIT

SQL	Pandas
select * from df_credit;	df_credit
select * from df_credit limit 3;	df_credit.head(3)
select [Approval Date] from df_credit where [Card Name]= 'Golden';	df_credit[df_credit['Card Name'] == 'Golden']['Approval Date']
select distinct [Card Name] from df_credit;	df_credit['Card Name'].unique()

SELECT with multiple conditions

select * from df_credit where [Card Name] = 'Golden' and [Credit Score] >= 750;	df_credit[(df_credit['Card Name'] == 'Golden') & (df_credit['Credit Score'] >= 750)]
select [First Name], [Last Name], [Credit Score], [Credit Approval] from df_credit where [Card Name] = 'Golden' and [Credit Score] >= 750;	df_credit[df_credit['Card Name'] == 'Golden') & (df_credit['Credit Score'] >= 750)][['First Name', 'Last Name', 'Credit Score', 'Credit Approval']]

ORDER BY

select * from df_credit where [Card Name] = 'Golden' order by [Credit Score];	df_credit[df_credit['Card Name'] == 'Golden'].sort_values('Credit Score')
select * from df_credit where [Card Name] = 'Golden' order by [Credit Score] desc;	df_credit[df_credit['Card Name'] == 'Golden'].sort_values('Credit Score', ascending=False)

IN... NOT IN

select *
from df_credit
where [Card Name] in ('Golden', 'Silver');

df_credit[df_credit['Card Name'].isin(['Golden', 'Silver'])]

select *
from df_credit
where [Card Name] not in ('Golden', 'Silver');

df_credit[~df_credit['Card Name'].isin(['Golden', 'Silver'])]

GROUP BY, COUNT, ORDER BY

select ([Card Name]),
    count (*)
from df_credit
group by [Card Name];

df_credit.groupby(['Card Name']).size()

select ([Card Name]),
    count (*)
from df_credit
group by [Card Name]
order by [Card Name],
    count (*) desc;

df_credit.groupby(['Card Name',]).size().to_frame('size').reset_index().sort_values(['Card Name', 'size'], ascending=[True, False])

110

HAVING

```
select [Card Name],
       count (*)
from df_credit
group by [Card Name]
having count (*) >= 2
order by count (*) desc;
```

```
df_credit.groupby('Card Name').filter(lambda g: len(g) >=
2).groupby('Card Name').size().sort_values(ascending=False)
```

```
select [Credit Score]
from df_credit
order by size desc limit 3;
```

Top N records

```
df_credit.nlargest(3, columns='Credit Score')
```

```
select [Credit Score]
from df_credit
order by size desc limit 3 offset 3;
```

```
df_credit.nlargest(3, columns='Credit Score').tail(3)
```

Aggregate functions (MIN, MAX, MEAN)

```
select max([Credit Score]),
       min([Credit Score]),
       avg([Credit Score]),
       median([Credit Score])
from runways;
```

```
df_credit.agg({'Credit Score': ['min', 'max', 'mean', 'median']})
```

JOIN

```
select [First Name],
       [Last Name],
       [Card Name],
       [Card Number]
from df_credit
join df_cards
   on (df_credit.[First Name] = df_cards.[First
Name] and
       df_credit.[Last Name] = df_cards.[Last
Name] )
where  df_credit.[Card Name] = 'Golden';
```

```
df_credit[df_credit['Card Name']==
'Golden'].merge(df_cards, on= ['First Name', 'Last
Name'])[['First Name', 'Last Name', 'Card Name', 'Card
Number']]
```

UNION ALL and UNION

```
select [First Name], [Last Name]
from df_credit
where [Card Name] = 'Golden'
union all
select [First Name], [Last Name]
from df_credit
where [Card Name] = 'Silver';
```

```
pd.concat([df_credit[df_credit['Card Name'] = 'Golden'][[ 'First Name', 'Last
Name']], df_credit[df_credit['Card Name'] = 'Silver'][[ 'First Name', 'Last
Name']]] )
```

CREATE TABLE

create table temp (id integer, col_1 text, col_2 text);	temp = pd.DataFrame(columns=['id','col_1','col_2'])

INSERT

insert into df_credit values ('Harry', 'Potter');	df_credit = df_credit.append(pd.DataFrame(np.array([['Harry', 'Potter']]), columns=['First Name', 'Last Name']) , sort=False)

UPDATE

update df_credit set [Credit Score] = 850 where [First Name]= 'Jacky';	df_credit.loc[df_credit['First Name'] == 'Jacky', 'Credit Score'] = 850

DELETE

delete from df_credit where [Card Name]= 'Golden';	df_credit = df_credit[df_credit['Card Name'] != 'Golden'] df_credit.drop(df_credit[df_credit['Card Name'] == 'Golden'].index)

Chapter 7   Visualizing Your Data

Data visualization is an essential tool and technique used to summarize and represent data graphically. Through expressing data with charts, graphs, and maps, data visualization provides a visual and intuitive way to look at and understand trends, patterns and outliers in data, and helps data scientists make data-driven decisions. The Python ecosystem provides dozers of visualization libraries and offers many different features including interactive, live, or highly customizable plots. This chapter will briefly introduce you to creating basic plots using Matplotlib and the Pandas visualization package.

7.1 Matplotlib

Matplotlib is one of the most popular and powerful python plotting libraries built on NumPy. It leverages the pyplot module, a collection of command style functions that make matplotlib like Matlab, to easily create line charts, bar charts, histograms, and more graphs.

To draw a plot using Matplotlib, you'll need know these fundamental parts of a Matplotlib plot: The figure, axes, axis, and artist. Below are their definitions.

- **Figure:** the topmost layer of the plot.
  The figure works as a canvas which contains subplots. A figure may contain one or more axes (subplots), sub axis, titles, subtitles, legends, and all contents of the plot.
- **Axes:** the subplot of the figure.
  The Axes defines a subplot and controls every detail inside of the subplot. Each Axes has a title, an x-label, y-label, and the type of graph.
- **Axis:** The axis defines the graph limits of the plot.

114

- **Artist:** Most Artists are tied to Axes. Everything which one can see on the figure is an artist. This can include text objects such as the title, legend, etc..

Below is a simple plot using matplotlib to show the relationship between "Credit Score" and "Income" in DataFrame df_credit. It's incredibly simple!

```
import matplotlib.pyplot as plt
y = list(df_credit['Credit Score'])
x = list(df_credit['Income'])
plt.plot(x, y)
```

out:

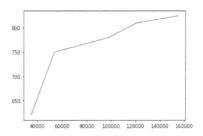

Matplotlib provides many types of plot and each includes different arguments according to its characteristics. The table below lists the common plot types and their arguments.

Plot Type	Function	Arguments
Line graph	plt.plot()	(x_data, y_data)
Scatter plot	plt.scatter()	(x_data, y_data)
Bar chart	plt.bar()	(x_locs, bar_heights, width)
Histogram	plt.hist()	(data, bins = int)
Pie chart	plt.pie()	(data, labels = list)

The following example shows how to use matplotlib to make a scatter plot with customized artists. The code follows common steps to make a plot: First pass data to a plot, then customize the plot with a title and labels.

115

```
import matplotlib.pyplot as plt
plt.scatter('Income','Credit Score',data=df_credt)
plt.xlabel('Income')
plt.ylabel('Credit Score')
plt.suptitle('Credit Score vs. Income')
plt.show()
```

out:

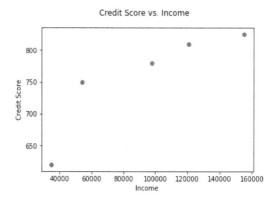

Note that there are two ways to pass data to a plot and they both accomplish the same task:

1. Converting a DataFrame column into a list, then assigning the lists directly to the axis' x and y components.
2. Passing the DataFrame to the 'data' argument, then specifying which columns are the x and y components.

```
plt.scatter('Income','Credit Score',data=df_credt)

# It is equivalent to

y = list(df_credt['Credit Score'])
x = list(df_credt['Income'])
plt.scatter(x,y)
```

7.2 Pandas Visualization

Pandas Visualization is an easier approach to create plots for Pandas DataFrames, since it creates plots using a simple wrapper around matplotlib's *plot()* function. Therefore, you don't need as much code as you would if you were creating plots directly using matplotlib. Pandas Visualization is implemented by the Pandas built in function, *plot()*, which includes many arguments for the purpose of all kinds of plots. If you'd like to know more about the detailed arguments, you may refer to the Pandas official documentation.

```
plot(x, y, kind, ax, subplots, sharex, sharey, layout, figsize, use_index, title, gri
d, legend, style, logx, logy, loglog, xticks, yticks, xlim, ylim, rot, fontsize, colo
rmap, table, yerr, xerr, secondary_y, sort_columns, **kwds)

Argument:
    kind: plot type {'bar', 'barh', 'pie', 'scatter', 'kde' etc}
    linestyle: line style {'solid', 'dotted', 'dashed'} (applies to line graph only)
    xlim, ylim: specify a tuple (lower limit, upper limit) of current axes
    legend: a Boolean value to display or hide the legend
    labels: descriptive legend  name for the columns in the DataFrame
    title: the string title of the plot
```

The Pandas built-in function, *plot()*, has a shortcut format which eliminates the need to specify the "kind" parameter. The general syntax for this format is *your_df.plot.<kind>()*, where *<kind>* is the kind of plot. The example below shows how to use the shortcut function *plot.scatter()* to create the same scatter plot as you would using the *plot()* wrapper function included in Pandas. You can see that the plots are the exact same, but the code is simpler and much more readable.

```
df_credit.plot( kind = 'scatter', x='Income',y='Credit Score',title='Credit Score
vs. Income')
```

```
# It is equivalent to the shortcut format
df_credit.plot.scatter(x='Income',y='Credit Score',title='Credit Score vs.
Income')
```

out:

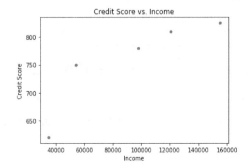

Another common plot made using the built-in function *plot()* is bar-chart showing the count of each type of credit card in df_credit. The code first counts unique values using the *value_count()* method on the "Card Name" column, then plots the results to a bar chart with title of 'Issued Cards'.

```
df_credt['Card Name'].value_counts().plot.bar(title = 'Issued Cards')
```

out:

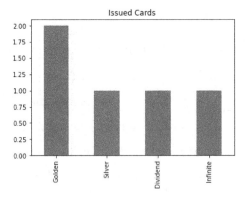

Chapter 8　Writing Programming Code with Python

Up until now, you've learned how to manipulate, summarize, and visualize data using Pandas and Matplotlib. If you haven't realized yet, all of these jobs are done statically, an example being DataFrames, where all columns are fixed. In the real world, however, you'd need to make Pandas process data dynamically and flexibly according to specific requirements handed to you. Thus, you'll need leverage the power of python, a high-level, interpreted, interactive, and object-oriented scripting language. In this chapter, you'll learn the basic syntax of Python, and one use case on how to make Pandas work with Python to achieve the goal of manipulating and analyzing data in the real world.

8.1 Basic Python Syntax

Python is a case sensitive programming language. It allows the identifier to start with any uppercase or lower case letter, or an underscore (_), followed by none or more letters, underscores and digits (0 to 9). However, you may not start an identifier name with numbers. Python also does not allow punctuation characters such as @, $, and % within identifiers.

Python rigidly enforces the use of indentation to mark blocks of code for flow control, functions, and classes. Accordingly, all statements within a block must be indented the same amount, and all continuous lines indented with same number of spaces would form a block. Python uses the single ('), double (") and triple (''' or """) quotes to denote string literals, where the single and double quotes are used for single line strings, and triple quotes are used for multiline strings. As well, Python uses the line continuation character (\) to denote that the next line continues the current statement, except the data types that are contained within the [], {}, or () brackets.

Python is a completely object-oriented language, meaning every variable in Python is an object. You do not need to declare variables nor their type before using them. A variable's declaration happens automatically when you assign a value to the variable using the equal sign (=).

Python has the following standard and built-in data types: Numeric, Boolean, String, List, Tuple, and Dictionary. Strings, lists, and tuples are sequence types which contain an ordered collection of similar or different data types, and use the index operator ([]) to access specific variables in the sequence. Dictionary objects are unordered collections of data which contain a key and value pairs, where each value can be fetched by their associated key.

Like other languages, Python also provides generic arithmetic operators (+ Addition, - Subtraction, * Multiplication, / Division, % Modulus, ** Exponent), comparison operators (==, !=, <>, >, <, >=, <=), logical operators (not, and, or), membership operators (in, not in) which are used to test membership in a sequence, and identity operators (is, not is) which are used to compare the memory locations of two objects.

8.2 Python Flow Control Statement

All programing languages have control flow to set the order in which a program code executes. In Python, control flow is regulated using conditional statements, loops, and function calls.

If-then-else conditions:

To conditionally execute blocks of statements, Python uses the compound statement *if*, which includes *if*, *elif*, and *else* clauses, where the **elif** and **else** clauses are optional. Here is the syntax of the **if** statement:

```
if condition1 :
    ForTrueCondition1
elif condition2 :
    ForTrueCondition2
elif condition3 :
    ForTrueCondition3
else:
    ForConditionFalse
```

loops:

Python provides **for loop** and **while loop** statements which allow you execute a group of statements multiple times. The **for loop** is used to repeatedly execute a piece of code an explicit number of times. The **while loop** will continue to loop as long as a condition is met. Here are two examples of how to print all numbers from 1 to 10 using a for loop and a while loop respectively.

for loop:

```
for id in range(1, 11): # range(start, stop) counts from start to stop-1
    print(id)
```

while loop:

```
id = 1
while id <= 10:
    print(id)
    id = id + 1
```

Python provides loop control statements to change execution orders from its normal sequence. The **break** statement terminates a loop statement, the **continue** statement terminates the current iteration of the loop body and continues execution with the next iteration, and the **pass** statement works as a placeholder for when a statement is syntactically required but no execution is needed.

Break statement:

```
while True:            # this loop can never terminate naturally
    x = 1
    print (x)
    x = x+1
    if x >1:
        break          # this loop terminates after printing 1
```

Continue statement:

```
for x in range(6):
    if x < 4:
        continue     # this loop terminates the loop when x < 4
    print (x)
```

Pass statement:

```
x = 10
if x < 5:
    print ('x is less than 5')
elif x < 20:
    pass                 # nothing to be done in this case
else:
    print('x is greater than 20')
```

8.3 Python User Defined Functions

A user defined function is a block of code that you can call and reuse for performing a pre-defined action, with the option of returning an output(s). In Python, the function is always followed by parentheses, and must be defined using keyword def. The example below defines a function named my_function, which prints "This is my first function" when you call it.

```
def my_function():
    print("This is my first function")
```

To call this function, just use the function name and pass any associated arguments. Since my_functin() has no arguments required, all you need to do is call the name without any arguments.

```
my_function()
```

out:

This is my first function

To require arguments for a function, put the argument(s) inside of the parenthesis, and separate them using commas. Note that you must pass all required arguments when calling a function. The example below prints your full name.

```
def my_function(first_name, last_name):
    print("Your name is: ", first_name, last_name)
my_function("Jacky", "Bai")
my_function("Henry", "Tu")
```

out:

Your name is: Jacky Bai

Your name is: Henry Tu

8.4 Python Script and Module

The Python interpreter can work on two basic modes: interactive and script. The interactive mode interactively executes Python statements submitted, and immediately returns the outputs for the line(s) of code executed. This mode is convenient for when you are experimenting with portions of code, and constantly need to make minor changes to lines. The script mode is the mode where written Python code is saved to .py files, where it can later be run by the Python interpreter. This mode is commonly used when business logic is complicated, and the python programs have multiple files, or long lines of code.

Like other programming languages, Python conventionally uses the *main()* function as a starting point in the program. In your program, an if statement where __*name*__ equals *"__main__"* will denote the beginning of the program. A simple example of *main()* function is shown below.

```python
def main():
    print("Hello World!")

if __name__ == "__main__":
main()
```

If we save the file as hello.py, we can run it using the command line as such:

```
python hello.py
```

out:

```
Hello World!
```

Usually, a plain Python program that is intended to be directly executed is called a Python **script**. As a Python program grows larger and becomes difficult to maintain, you may use **module**s to split it into several files for easier maintenance and reusability. A **module** can include variables, functions, and classes, as well as runnable code. It is intended to be imported by another program to use its functionality. After importing the module, you may use any of its classes, functions, or variables that are accessible to you.

For example, you may have a module named added.py which includes the following function.

```
def add(x,y):
    return x+y
```

To access the modules contents, you must first import it, and from thereon you may use any of the properties provided. For instance, to use the *add()* function of the module *added*, call added.add()

```
import added
added = added.add(5,6)
print(added)
```

out:

11

8.5 A Use Case of Pandas

This use case is designed to demonstrate how to dynamically process DataFrames using Pandas and Python, and to show how modules are called in other modules and how they work together. This use case continues to use the same datasets we've been working with earlier: Credit, Cards and Transactions. The program has 4 modules: describing, processing, output and

125

the credit (main). Each part contains a detailed description of the module and source code.

1. describing.py

Module describing (describing.py) simply describes the DataFrames we have, including the shapes of the datasets, the columns' names, data types, missing records, and common statistics of the numerical columns. Finally, these results are outputted to a plain text file.

```python
import pandas as pd

def describing(df_in, df_name, txt_file):

    shape = df_in.shape
    df_info = pd.DataFrame(df_in.dtypes).reset_index()
    df_info.columns = ['Column Name','Data Type']
    df_null_cnt = df_in.count()
    df_info['Missing'] = shape[0] - df_null_cnt
    df_describe = df_in.describe()
    df_T = df_describe.T.reset_index()
    df_T.rename(columns={'index': 'Column Name'}, inplace=True)
    df_info = df_info.merge(df_T, how= 'left', on= 'Column Name')
    df_info.rename(columns={'index': 'Column Name', '0': 'Data
Type'}, inplace=True)

    with open(txt_file, "a" ) as text_file:
        print("===================================================",
file=text_file)
        print(df_name + ' : has the shape of ' + str(shape) ,
file=text_file)
        print(df_name + "'s simple profiling is as below",
file=text_file)
        print (df_info, file=text_file )

    return df_info
```

2. processing.py

Module processing (processing.py) merges two Dataframes inputted by common attributes to obtain a new merged DataFrame. This is done by combining clients and transactions through Card Number, then computes required aggregated statistics for each group of the generated merged DataFrame.

```python
import pandas as pd
import numpy as np

def transactions(df_credit, df_cards, df_transactions):

    df_credit_cards = df_credit.merge(df_cards, how = "inner",
on=['First Name', 'Last Name'])
    df_credit_cards.drop_duplicates(['First Name', 'Last Name'],
keep='last', inplace=True )
    df_trans = df_credit_cards.merge(df_transactions, how =
"inner", on=['Card Number'])
    df_trans = df_trans[['First Name', 'Last Name', 'Card Name',
'Card Number', 'Date', 'Transactions', 'Amount' ]]
    return df_trans


def grouping(df_in, group, features, funcs ):
    df_out = df_in.groupby(group,
as_index=False)[features].agg(funcs)
    df_out.reset_index(inplace=True)
    df_out.rename(columns={'index': group}, inplace=True)
    df_out.columns = ['_'.join(x).rstrip('_') for x in
df_out.columns.ravel()]
    return df_out
```

3. output.py

Module output (output.py) outputs the aggregated results as a graphical plot and as a csv file.

```python
import pandas as pd
import matplotlib.pyplot as plt

def out_plot(df_in, kind, x, y, fig_out):
    plot = df_in.plot( kind = kind, x= x, y=y, title=x + ' vs. ' +
y)
    fig = plot.get_figure()
    fig.savefig(fig_out)
    plt.show()


def out_csv(df_in, csv_file):
    df_in.to_csv(csv_file)
```

4. Credit.py

The main program performs the four following actions in order:

1. First, it loads the three datasets.
2. Next, it calls the describing module to describe the data loaded.
3. Then, it calls the processing module to merge the inputted datasets and get aggregated statistics of each group from the merged dataset.
4. Finally, it calls the module output to export the results to a .csv file and a .png file for the data and plot respectively.

```
5. import pandas as pd
   import describing
   import processing
   import numpy as np
   import output
   import sys
   import os

   def main():
       df_credit, df_cards, df_transactions = data_input()
       l_group, kind, l_feature, l_func, figures, fig_out,
   csv_file, txt_file = read_para(sys.argv)

       for df_in in ['df_credit', 'df_cards',
   'df_transactions']:
           df_desc = profiling(locals()[df_in], df_in,
   txt_file)

       df_trans = processing.transactions(df_credit, df_cards,
   df_transactions)
       df_group = processing.grouping(df_trans, l_group,
   l_feature, l_func)

       output.out_plot(df_group, kind, l_group, figures,
   fig_out)
       output.out_csv(df_group, csv_file)


   def data_input():
       url_credit =
   'https://raw.githubusercontent.com/billbai0102/Pandas-
```

```
Book/master/credit.csv'
    url_cards =
'https://raw.githubusercontent.com/billbai0102/Pandas-
Book/master/cards.csv'
    url_trans =
'https://raw.githubusercontent.com/billbai0102/Pandas-
Book/master/transactions.csv'

    df_credit=pd.read_csv(url_credit, parse_dates =
['Approval Date'])
    df_cards=pd.read_csv(url_cards, parse_dates =
['Effective Date'])
    df_transactions=pd.read_csv(url_trans, parse_dates =
['Date'])
    return df_credit, df_cards, df_transactions


def profiling(df_in, name_df, txt_file):
    df_desc = describing.describing(df_in, name_df,
txt_file)
    return df_desc


def read_para(argvs):
    l_group = argvs[1]
    kind = argvs[2]
    l_feature = argvs[3]
    l_func = argvs[4]
    figurs = argvs[5]
    fig_out = argvs[6]
    csv_file = argvs[7]
    txt_file = argvs[8]
    l_feature = list(l_feature.strip(' []').split(','))
    l_func = list(l_func.strip('" []').split(','))
    l_func = [eval(x) for x in l_func]

    if os.path.exists(txt_file):
        os.remove(txt_file)

    return  l_group, kind, l_feature, l_func, figurs,
fig_out, csv_file, txt_file


if __name__ == "__main__":
    main()
```

Parameters:

sys.argv [1]: the list for group name for aggregations
sys.argv [2]: kind of the plot
sys.argv [3]: the list of feature names for the group aggregations
sys.argv [4]: the list of statistics functions for the group aggregations
sys.argv [5]: the list of the y-label in the plot
sys.argv [6]: the file name of plot
sys.argv [7]: the csv file name for the results of aggregation
sys.argv [8]: the text file name for data describing

Below are the running results of the two scenarios, where each scenario is given different inputs. From this, you may observe how modules work together in a batch running mode. It is encouraged that you play with the code to gain an in-depth understanding of how they can work in a real project.

Scenario 1:

In the first scenario, we run the code for exporting the bar chart for the total transactions count for each Card Name. We also export the data-describing summary and aggregated results by each Card Name.

```
python.exe "credit.py" "Card Name" "bar" [Transactions,Amount]
[np.sum,np.mean] "Transactions_sum" "C:/Pandas/Samples/output.png"
"C:/Pandas/Samples/output.csv" "C:/Pandas/Sample/profile.txt"
```

Output:

1. Output.csv

	Card Name	Transactions_sum	Transactions_mean	Amount_sum	Amount_mean
0	Golden	8	2	220.45	55.1125
1	Infinite	11	3.666666667	1178.1	392.7
2	Silver	10	3.333333333	97.4	32.46666667

2. Output.png

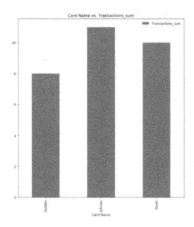

3. profile.txt

```
================================================
df_credit : has the shape of (5, 7)
df_credit's simple profiling is as below
        Column Name    Data Type  Missing  ...        50%        75%        max
0       First Name       object       NaN  ...        NaN        NaN        NaN
1        Last Name       object       NaN  ...        NaN        NaN        NaN
2     Credit Score        int64       NaN  ...     780.00     810.00     825.00
3  Credit Approval         bool       NaN  ...        NaN        NaN        NaN
4        Card Name       object       NaN  ...        NaN        NaN        NaN
5           Income      float64       NaN  ...   98000.58  120800.88  155000.62
6    Approval Date  datetime64[ns]    NaN  ...        NaN        NaN        NaN

[7 rows x 11 columns]
================================================
df_cards : has the shape of (6, 5)
df_cards's simple profiling is as below
        Column Name    Data Type  Missing  ...     50%      75%      max
0       First Name       object       NaN  ...     NaN      NaN      NaN
1        Last Name       object       NaN  ...     NaN      NaN      NaN
2      Card Number       object       NaN  ...     NaN      NaN      NaN
3       Limitation        int64       NaN  ...  9900.0  11500.0  15000.0|
4   Effective Date  datetime64[ns]    NaN  ...     NaN      NaN      NaN

[5 rows x 11 columns]
================================================
df_transactions : has the shape of (10, 4)
df_transactions's simple profiling is as below
      Column Name    Data Type  Missing  count  ...    25%   50%      75%    max
0     Card Number       object       NaN    NaN  ...    NaN   NaN      NaN    NaN
1            Date  datetime64[ns]    NaN    NaN  ...    NaN   NaN      NaN    NaN
2    Transactions        int64       NaN   10.0  ...  2.000   3.0   3.7500    5.0
3          Amount      float64       NaN   10.0  ... 26.275  40.2  103.6825  785.0

[4 rows x 11 columns]
```

Scenario 2:

In this scenario, we run the code to export a pie chart for the total transactions Amount by each clients' First Name. We also export the data-describing summary and aggregated results by each First Name.

```
python.exe " credit.py" "First Name" "pie" [Transactions,Amount]
[np.sum,np.mean] "Amount_sum" "C:/Pandas/Samples/output.png"
"C:/Pandas/Samples/output.csv" "C:/Pandas/Sample/profile.txt
```

Output:

1. Ouput.csv

	First Name	Transactions_sum	Transactions_mean	Amount_sum	Amount_mean
0	Desmond	10	3.333333	97.4	32.46667
1	Henry	3	1.5	76.35	38.175
2	Jacky	11	3.666667	1178.1	392.7
3	Jane	5	2.5	144.1	72.05

2. Output.png

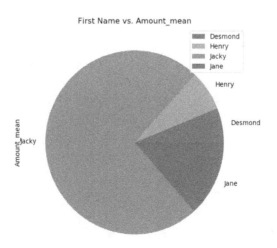

3. profile.txt

```
=================================================
df_credit : has the shape of (5, 7)
df_credit's simple profiling is as below
        Column Name     Data Type  Missing  ...        50%         75%          max
0      First Name          object      NaN  ...        NaN         NaN          NaN
1       Last Name          object      NaN  ...        NaN         NaN          NaN
2    Credit Score           int64      NaN  ...     780.00      810.00       825.00
3 Credit Approval            bool      NaN  ...        NaN         NaN          NaN
4       Card Name          object      NaN  ...        NaN         NaN          NaN
5          Income         float64      NaN  ...   98000.58   120800.88    155000.62
6   Approval Date  datetime64[ns]      NaN  ...        NaN         NaN          NaN

[7 rows x 11 columns]
=================================================
df_cards : has the shape of (6, 5)
df_cards's simple profiling is as below
        Column Name     Data Type  Missing  ...     50%      75%       max
0      First Name          object      NaN  ...     NaN      NaN       NaN
1       Last Name          object      NaN  ...     NaN      NaN       NaN
2     Card Number          object      NaN  ...     NaN      NaN       NaN
3      Limitation           int64      NaN  ...  9900.0  11500.0  15000.0|
4  Effective Date  datetime64[ns]      NaN  ...     NaN      NaN       NaN

[5 rows x 11 columns]
=================================================
df_transactions : has the shape of (10, 4)
df_transactions's simple profiling is as below
      Column Name     Data Type  Missing  count  ...     25%    50%       75%    max
0    Card Number          object      NaN    NaN  ...     NaN    NaN       NaN    NaN
1           Date  datetime64[ns]      NaN    NaN  ...     NaN    NaN       NaN    NaN
2   Transactions           int64      NaN   10.0  ...   2.000    3.0    3.7500    5.0
3         Amount         float64      NaN   10.0  ...  26.275   40.2  103.6825  785.0

[4 rows x 11 columns]
```

*Since the inputted datasets are same, the profile.txt is exactly same as scenario 1

Index